MW00879376

This is a work of non-fiction. Names, characters, businesses, places, events and incidents are either the products of the author's memory or based on gathered statistical information.

The author has tried to recreate events, locales and conversations from his memories of them. In order to maintain their anonymity in some instances the author has changed the names of individuals and places. The author may have changed some identifying characteristics and details such as physical properties, occupations and places of residence.

This book is not intended as a substitute for the medical advice of physicians. The reader should regularly consult a physician in matters relating to his/her health and particularly with respect to any symptoms that may require diagnosis or medical attention.

"A person who fails after making an honest-to-goodness attempt at suicide is a double loser. First because they tried killing themselves, and second because they couldn't even get that right."

(Jim Goad, 2014)

chapter one

The first time I seriously tried to stop my pain was in 2015. The sieving pain ravaged my mind day after day. At night, when my thoughts should be stilled, the anguish forced its way into my sleep. On this rainy evening, both my hands gripped the top of the steering wheel. Valerie's hazel eyes did a poor job of concealing the terror within them. She clung onto her long, reddish blonde hair like a little girl unwilling to give up her favorite doll.

Valerie and I had met online in 2012 and immediately fell deeply in love. She was now my fiancée and her introverted, calm personality was a great counterpoint to my extroverted and boisterous nature. We quickly found ourselves living together and our first few years had been storybook perfect – romantic hikes, spontaneous road trips, and world traveling. But now this nightmare was both of our daily realities.

As I took the rolling right-hand turn onto the highway, I began screaming at the top of my lungs. Havoc had come knocking. My tumultuous mind replayed an inmate's prison-issued white shoes stomping on my face, over and over and over again. I had just experienced a number of flashbacks, which were the scariest damn things – re-witnessing a sudden and frightful memory of an event from the past. It is reliving a memory that you debunked and wished away, right down to the finest detail. It is impossible in these moments to know what is real and what the mind is cruelly creating. Valerie was doing the best she could to return my sanity as my right foot pushed the accelerator as far down as it could go.

"Jamie, you are going to be okay! I promise you. Please calm down!" she pleaded again and again with panic increasing in her voice as the odometer shuttered. "We will get through this together."

Her words only made my blood squeal louder. I had the throttle down as hard as it could go – I felt my toes throbbing as they reached their maximum extension. The wheel shook in my hands and my feet pulsated. Valerie yelled and warm wind flew in through the rear windows. It was just 700 meters after hastily entering the freeway that we came across an emergency-only turn-around and quickly began heading westbound into eastbound traffic, our bodies swinging left and then quickly back right as the tires screeched and we corrected back onto the road. The smell of the tire rubber and the engine was pungent – burnt yet sweet. Valerie yelled, I yelled, and the engine screamed.

"Please Jamie, do not do this!" she shrieked. She reached out for anything that could potentially stop what was about to happen. "At least don't kill innocent people. Or me!" she begged as one would when they felt their last breath approaching.

It was those words that resonated deep inside me. Her plea raced through my brain. Why was I risking the innocent just because I wanted to die? The very thought made me hate myself even more. My head drooped shamefully as I pulled the smoking Kia onto a grassy area at the side of the freeway. Both of our faces were covered with tears and fear. Our eyes met, each asking the same desperate question – what the hell was wrong with me?

chapter two

This book is more for me than it is for you. Nonetheless, you have found yourself, one way or another, reading these words as I write them. My pen hits the pad of paper, and you read the words I put together. It is quite amazing, actually. From the left moving right, from the top of one page to the bottom of the next, you and I make our way. Sometimes at a pace that feels painfully slow as my mind gets hung up on flashbacks so real that I can smell the prison walls of my past. At other times so frantically and exhausting that I am more of a man under attack than a writer. My publisher, one day, will tell me that you want action, that my story is too slow or too boring for the average reader. They will tell me that you want to be excited, stupefied and forced to gasp for air as you read my words. They will say to me "You need more blood. More violence! More death!". Tell them about a stabbing!" they will suggest to me. "Or what death smells like. Tell them what it sounds like when brain matter splatters on concrete. Tell them!"

And, yes, I will tell you these things. But just like misery, it takes time. It builds up. It doesn't happen overnight and you cannot skip ahead. There are clear and precise steps to utter misery. Undefined phases. Indeterminate stages. And I have gone through them all. I will start where it all began eight years ago. Stage One. The beginning: Flowers, Rainbows, Promise, and Happiness.

I was your typical kid and good at most things I put a little effort into. I played little league baseball in my hometown of Surrey, British Columbia in the Pacific Northwest. This began with tee-ball as a young five year old boy and continued all the way up to competitive teams when I was a lanky 16 year old teenager. I was incredibly proud to be voted team captain and it was an honor I was eager to live up to. From a very early age I had loved to be a leader, and this inner strength grew stronger as the years passed. In high school, I began taking Advanced Placement classes and encouraging my schoolmates to follow along. I learned to lead by example, often using humor to avoid conflicts and to obtain results. This jovial demeanour quickly became something I was well known for – a jokester, a class clown, a speaker at events and weddings. I woke up with a smile each morning and went to bed looking forward to the next day. Life was good.

My adventure in corrections started with a sharp slap on the back. It was spring of 2007 and my then girlfriend's mother had hit me with a newspaper advertisement she had come across that morning. It was a government advertisement for a position with Corrections. 'Reduce Reoffending and Protect Communities' the brightly colored advertisement read. At the time I wasn't looking for work, but my future mother-in-law made it clear that I should be. My parents of course agreed. I had grown up in a middle-class household as the youngest of three children, and my childhood had been relatively easy. My sister became a high school teacher, my brother a high school vice-principal and my father worked as a government employee as well, as a postal carrier. My mother took care of the household and cared for us children. I had always dreamt of becoming a police officer, and from an early age my friends were very aware of my fascination with law enforcement. In early high school, I had already looked into the basic qualifications I would have to meet and started to plan for how I might fulfill each and every one of them. But unlike most prepubescent boys who play cops and robbers and have dreams of catching bad guys, I never grew out of this childhood fantasy.

I put in my application with the Royal Columbian Mounted Police (RCMP) at the tender age of 19 – still essentially a boy. I had diligently completed a couple of years of post- secondary schooling at a local University which was something I knew the RCMP sought in candidates. My criminology degree is what I had begun working away at as well as minoring in both sociology and psychology. I also had over a decade of playing team sports behind me, something else I knew they saw as a strength. And if nothing else, I had passion. This is something I knew would show through and hopefully set me apart from other applicants. I wanted this. Unfortunately, my application was unsuccessful. They explained that it was because of my lack of life experience. They encouraged me to apply again however, after I had taken some time to gain the life experience that I was lacking at such a young age. They suggested that I travel and learn about other cultures and that I maybe further my education and ideally complete my degree.   Primarily, they asked that I become accomplished in some different jobs in order to learn some skills that I could bring to the RCMP to make myself a better officer when the time came. They also mentioned the benefits of volunteering with the RCMP and so I did just that. I began volunteering with my local RCMP detachment shortly after I was turned down as a police constable. I volunteered once a week and thoroughly enjoyed getting out in the community and helping the public. Some weeks, we would leave notices on vehicles encouraging the owners to keep their cars more secure. Other weeks I would work from the detachment, dealing with the public as they came in to file complaints, pick up lost items or complete other various tasks. It would take time to achieve my dream; the hundreds of volunteer hours would take months, if not years, to accumulate.

However, that slap on the back from my girlfriend's mother changed my life forever.

The Government Correctional Service advertisement showed three men and one woman dressed in inspiring law enforcement uniforms, complete with the duty belt I was accustomed to seeing police officers wear. I had dreamt of wearing one of those belts ever since a police officer gave a presentation to my grade two class. After the presentation, we gathered around the police officer, thirty little bodies clamoring over each other trying to ask questions and giggling. My usual boisterous personality was completely overcome by awe. I silently wiggled through the crowd to admire his duty belt and even tried to touch the rough black fabric before he casually brushed my hand away.

What was it that drew me so strongly to careers in law enforcement? This became a question I continually found stirring internally with very few clear answers. Was it the power of the position? The respect the uniform garnered from the public? Or perhaps it was my urge to continually save the day. I could never put my finger on it exactly, but I have a strong feeling that it was a combination of all of these attributes. In addition, I had a real desire to help others, especially the weak and those in crisis. I wanted to be my city's Batman, or Robin at least.

The look on the four correctional officers' faces in the advertisement was one of a general happiness. Two had large smiles, while the other two had controlled grins. The advertisement promised a great starting wage, a great benefit package and a shift pattern that I envisioned as being beneficial as it would give me lots of time to travel the world. But it was the faces of the correctional officers in that advertisement that really pulled me in; they looked so powerful. They showed a confidence I had secretly lacked for so long.

Within a few flips of the calendar pages, I found myself in the middle of the hiring process with the Correctional Services. The process was lengthy and included extensive physical and personality testing as well as thorough background checks. Each step brought its own stresses and worries, but advancing through each stage also elicited enormous gratification. Sharing these experiences with my family and tight-knit friend group was immensely satisfying. My family was happy to see me chasing my dreams and my friends constantly exclaimed how proud they were of me.

A short six months later, I received a letter from the warden informing me that I had passed all the steps of the recruiting process. I was therefore accepted into the Correctional Training Program. Over the following ten weeks, my recruit class learned everything there was to know about being a correctional officer in Canada. This included the history of corrections, the laws governing correctional officers, and the day-to-day policies and procedures we would need to become familiar with. We learned how to talk with inmates in non-combative ways using their slang to maintain a certain peace within the prison walls. We learned how to de-escalate situations verbally when issues broke out amongst the inmates and were taught how to read an inmate's body language. During a week-long physical training section of the program, we learned how to protect ourselves. We were informed that our prison did not use firearms, but some of us would be provided with batons and pepper spray depending on where in the prison we were posted. Our number-one personal defense tool, we were taught, was our PAL (Personal Alarm Locator). We would wear the PAL on our uniform lapel at all times. Pushing the red button on the top of the PAL would summon backup from all over the prison. It was meant to be used only in worst-case scenarios – inmate-on-staff assaults, inmate-on-inmate assaults and medical emergencies.

The weeks went by quickly and on the last day of class, upon passing all the tests, we were presented with our badges and sworn in as correctional officers. It was official. Two photographs were taken and the warden reached out to give me a formal handshake. I was now a certified peace officer in the province of British Columbia. My heart was full. I was proud. I was happy. I was ready. Or so I thought.

chapter three

The learning curve was steep. My class graduated on Friday and just two short days later on Sunday I was posted to one of the living units within one of the largest Pretrial Centers in all of Canada.

As a maximum security remand center, the Pretrial Center is the home of a vast demographic of inmates, including serial killers, terrorists and rapists. In the early 1990's, when the jail opened, there were a total of 150 inmate beds. At that time, each living unit averaged 10 inmates for every two correctional officers. When I got there in 2007, Canada's new 'tough on crime' laws had bogged down the court system, with multiple-year trial date delays. To say the least, the Pretrial Center was bursting at the seams as were prisons right across Canada and the United States. British Columbia's nine correctional centers averaged 140 percent occupancy, with individual centers ranging from 107 percent to 177 percent occupancy.

Of those in custody, a large percentage of prisoners were 'remanded' which means they had been accused of a serious federal Criminal Code offence, but denied bail. Therefore, they must await trial in a Provincial Correctional Centre such as the Pretrial Center. Though the average stay for a remanded inmate is just 33 days, some remained for the entire length of their long, complex trials; in some cases, taking five or more years. While about 80% of remanded individuals will eventually be convicted, they are all innocent until proven guilty, which means that, although they are offered programs and work activities, none can be required to work or attend group sessions. I quickly realized that remand centers are a fruitful recruiting ground for gangs and that this environment serves as a top of the line education program for future criminal behaviour. Boredom leads to talking and talking leads to learning and once they are out in the real world, they take these lessons to the street to commit more and more serious offenses.

The safety statistics started to wane quickly at the Pretrial Center and management could not keep up with the fact that its officers and inmates were being injured, maimed and dying at a level never seen before.

Between 2004 and 2016, there were 19 deaths at the Pretrial Center and hundreds more seriously injured. It had clearly surpassed a dangerous climax point; this was full-blown war. Staff and inmates sent to the Pretrial Center alive were going home maimed or worse. The situation was critical.

Doug Purdin, chair of the Corrections and Staff Services component of the B.C. Government and Services Employees' Union, said he "believed the government's statistics were conservative, and that union figures show 244 assaults against staff in the past five years at three correctional facilities alone."

Bunk beds were retrofitted into each of the cells to allow the maximum number of inmates to be incarcerated. "Fuck this, I want my own room," they would yell at me. "Campbell, leave me the last single bunked bed," they would demand. However, at the same time, government funding cuts in the Ministry of Justice lowered staffing numbers. Inmates on each living unit now maxed out at 72, and there was just one officer assigned to them. Perceptions were dangerous and emotions were tense. Violence was common and anticipated by both inmates and staff alike. Even while these struggles continued, the government now decided to move to an 'open living concept,' which removed secured staff stations and replaced them with insecure open desk areas situated in the center of the unit. The government's idea was to no longer just warehouse inmates but rather securely rehabilitate each inmate with various programing and services. To me, I felt like an animal on display in a zoo. Inmates who obviously had very little to do with their abundance of spare time took to monitoring the staff as a hobby. They picked up on our moods, overheard whispered conversations between coworkers and became familiar with our day to day behaviours. Inmates were unlocked throughout the day and permitted to move freely within the living unit, often circling the officers like sharks on blood. Management stated that its hands were tied and the officers were left to the wolves.

Staff assaults were fairly infrequent but it was just three weeks after being handed my badge that I faced my first attack. Without provocation, while I sat at my unprotected staff station, an inmate began shouting and yelling at me about conditions in the jail.

"Hey! Campbell! This is bullshit. Last time I was in here I had my own bed, my own cell and I didn't have to eat the shit you fuckers are feeding us. You expect me to live on this shit? They shouldn't even be feeding this to animals." He ranted, going on and on. And he was right, what they ate was a modified soy product shaped into various food staples and it probably shouldn't have even been fed to animals. But at this point he was acting like an animal although I didn't feel it was appropriate to draw the comparison.

The incident quickly escalated as he picked up a clear plastic juice container sitting on a table near him and threw it directly at me. I made a quick left juke like that of a football player and avoided having the container hit me in the head. As I had been trained just weeks beforehand in the Correctional Training Program, I initiated a code yellow by pushing the emergency panic transmitter I wore on my left lapel. The little red button on the top of our Personal Alarm System was all we had for requesting help because at this time, management had not provided us with personal portable radios. These would be provided only a year later, after another staff assault had occurred and the officer's PAL had malfunctioned.

My emergency call was received by our control officers. They dispatched assistance to my living unit. Two control officers worked in a special security pod called control and were responsible for all movements within the prison and for initiating responses in all sorts of emergencies. The physical harm to me this time was minimal; except for some red juice dripping down the white brick wall behind me, and a little on my face and uniform, I walked away unscathed. However, for the first time I realized I was not safe. I was reminded of this attack each shift, as management refused to clean the dried-up juice from the wall behind me. Month after month, I came to work and was brought back to the incident – the blood-like juice rejigged my memory of what had taken place. Inmates too, took notice. "Campbell, are they ever going to clean that for you?" an inmate asked months afterward. "Looks like shit," he continued. Four and a half months and multiple requests later, a painter visited the unit to remove that physical memory from my mind. And as he rolled the white paint over the red splatter, I felt a wave of relief come over me.

Life inside prison is highly tense; at all times, just a spark short of a wildfire. Staff and inmates alike walk on eggshells on a daily basis. Correctional Officers are constantly awaiting the next incident and inmates are trying to avoid becoming the next incident. Screams and shouts echo around the high cement ceilings, heavy steel doors constantly slam and arguments quickly lead to physical fights or stabbings. Assaults are common and breaking basic prison code comes with harsh penalties. For inmates, being reprimanded by correctional staff for basic infractions is far preferred to being disciplined in the showers by fellow inmates. Almost anything can be a reason for a beating: speaking to a correctional officer, touching something that is not yours, or even looking at the wrong person at the wrong time. Sometimes an inmate just doesn't have a chance.

On July 9, 2014, *The Georgia Straight,* a local newspaper, stated that Canada's correctional investigator had reported that assaults had risen to 636 serious assaults in 2012-13 just in Canadian prisons alone. The investigator noted that statistics for assault – especially sexual assault – were likely much higher than these statistics indicated. "Inmates tend to try to sort things out amongst themselves instead of involving the authorities in disputes," he said. "Suicides have remained fairly constant, at an average of nine per year. However, attempted suicides have risen dramatically to an all-time high of 113 in 2012-13."

Statistics regarding the use of segregation, which is where I would soon find myself working, were also documented. The documents contained lots of disturbing information, including an enormous increase in the number of inmates being held in segregation, which was supposed to be used only for the worst of the worst inmate population however "8,221 inmates were held in segregation in 2012-13 alone."

Each day in jail for a weak inmate is a roll of the dice, a flip of the coin. For these types of inmates who cannot make it in the general population, each prison has protective custody living units. Protective custody living units are identical to general population living units in size, shape and amenities, however, protective custody inmates are far below general population inmates in the prison hierarchy. Often, inmates accused of sexual offences, offences against women or children, or inmates who have

23

cooperated with law enforcement find themselves in protective custody. These inmates are often labeled "rats."

There were 102 inmate deaths in correctional facilities in British Columbia alone between 2004 and 2011, a large portion of these deaths were protective custody inmates.

In general, prison cells are not cozy; regardless whether one is assigned to general population or protective custody. The building is made entirely of steel and concrete and the coldness seems to sink into it all. Everything is hard and rigid, from the rules and attitudes to the bars and the cells. The slams of cell doors radiate throughout the prison and the echoes of televisions and arguments are overheard in each living unit. Moving around a prison itself takes a fair amount of work and time, as hallways are long concrete tunnels leading from one living area to the next. Every few meters is a door that can only be accessed by pressing the call button and voicing your inmate or staff name and where you are headed. Going through these controlled steel doors, from one side of the prison to the other, can be a time-consuming process for staff and inmate alike.

Daily life in prison is quite mundane and repetitive. Cell doors are opened at 0700hrs, and most inmates are anxious to get out of their 9-by-11-foot cells immediately. Breakfast is rolled into each living unit via a stainless steel padlocked cart, which is opened for the inmates by the living unit officer. Breakfast is served in airplane-style individual containers. This process is repeated again at lunch at 1100hrs and again for dinner at 1630hrs. The food menu has four rotations, so each month you will see the same food rotation only once. Inmates are forced to lock up into their cells for four short, regulated staff breaks throughout the day, and are then locked up for a final lockup at 2115hrs. Lights are completely out at 2130hrs and the noise in the living units at this point is usually non-existent. This entire process repeats itself the next morning at 0700hrs and never alternates, changes or varies except during times of emergency or during a lockdown. A lockdown is a wide-ranging term indicating a period when all inmates are locked in their cells up for an undetermined duration of time so that officers can investigate a crime or attempt to intervene in a breach of prison security. Often these are actions that staff have caught wind of; drugs moving through the prison, weapons rumored to be on a person or in a living unit, and escape plans are all examples of this. In prison, the unknown is scary and staff find safety in the repetition of each day. A good day for a Correctional Officer would be a day during which there was nothing to report.

Specially chosen inmates who had shown a long period of good behavior, usually in excess of a year, could sometimes apply for one of two inmate jobs that the Pretrial Centre offered. These jobs paid little, but to the inmate, being able to get outside the living unit that they had called home for months or years was priceless. The same grey walls. The same steel one-piece toilet cell sink. The same steel bedframe. The same food. The "same old, same old" became very old, very fast.

Inmate Bunson, a chubby inmate with a perfectly vertical scar separating his big bushy eyebrows headed over to me. He had been accepted the prior day to work in the maintenance shop and had a look of pride on his face that he was doing a lousy job of hiding. I had just finished yelling out all of the workers names to prepare them to leave the living unit. I had a good rapport with Bunson, and a simple respect for him. "Campbell, what does it say about me that I'm nervous about my first day of work, which they will be paying me pennies for?" he asked. I fired back with the first truth I could think of, "Because you would do just about anything at this point to get the hell off of this unit! At least for a bit and see what the rest of the world looks like" I continued jokingly.

He smirked back and as the door opened for the crew to leave, he gave me a head nod and wished me a good day in not so many words. The maintenance crew was still just a group of inmates, but even the correctional officers treated these individuals a little better. It went both ways, in fact. It was an unwritten and unspoken rule, but it worked for both sides of the equation. As for that morning, he wouldn't need to hear the living unit echoes and the fans turning on and off. The 7 a.m. breakfast call. Nothing. He was free for the day. Well, sort of. At the very least, off to see a different set of walls.

On a daily routine, medications are distributed to inmates throughout the prison in what is often a hectic but well-supervised process. Inmates who have proven to a doctor that they require medication are called out of the living unit into a spare hall. By showing their prison identification card to the nurse behind the glass, they are rewarded with a small cup holding the approved pills, creams or other medications that a doctor has prescribed them. Getting this approval is not an easy process; when the inmates are not approved, it often leads to fights and arguments with medical staff. Drug-seeking behavior is highly common in all jails, and I have experienced every type of manipulation known to man! It is rare for an inmate to get even basic cold and sinus medication because these products are often altered and taken in a way that allows the inmate to get a high from them. To prevent this, natural products or procedures are often encouraged. Sleep. Exercise. Drink more water. That sort of thing. And 99% of the time, not surprisingly, it fixed the problem.

In Summer 2010, various inmates began reporting very similar symptoms that had the doctor perplexed. Extreme nausea and light headedness was the common complaint. Blood work was taken and shortly afterward we realized that these inmates had been stealing the hand sanitizer pumps that were bolted onto the walls throughout the prison and were ingesting the alcohol from the product. We were amazed at their creativity but we were not overly shocked. Spending years upon years working in a prison, you learn that nothing can surprise you anymore. The mind of a man living in such a small and quarantined area with nothing but the most basic daily repetition creates the perfect storm for this type of inmate "creative behavior." It was shortly after this that all of the hand sanitizer dispensers were replaced with a foam product, that made it impossible to extract the alcohol like some inmates had previously been doing. The good guys won this 'battle' but it was just one of the constant games we played as the correctional officers tried to stay one step ahead of the inmates at all times.

Perhaps the most strictly guarded of medications that can be prescribed regularly in prison is methadone. Methadone is a synthetic analgesic drug that is similar to morphine in its effects but it is longer acting. Because of this, it is used as a substitute drug in the treatment of morphine and heroin addiction. In theory, it should slowly allow the addict to take lower and lower doses of the drug until he or she is no longer addicted to the opiate. However, in practice this is rarely, if ever, the case. Rather, it becomes a lifelong daily substitution for injected heroine and morphine. Either way, it does create an improvement in the safety of everyone involved, especially in a prison setting. Seven days a week, the approved methadone inmates were called from their living units and securely pat frisked. Then they received their methadone to drink, which is mixed with a tangy flavor juice. The inmates are mouth checked to confirm they have swallowed everything, and then taken to a side room in which they must remain for 15 minutes before returning to their cells back on their living unit. Because methadone replaces opioids and heroin, some inmates feel that by getting other inmates methadone, they could get a high, which is actually extremely dangerous and not true. Nonetheless, in fall 2010, we had an inmate who drank his prescribed methadone and, after his 15-minute wait in the mandatory waiting room, went to his cell and vomited it up. He then went on to strain the vomit with a basic strainer in order to separate the liquid he had just ingested to anything else that was in his stomach from the night prior. His cell mate drank the liquid and soon after became unresponsive and extremely ill. He was rushed to hospital and it was quickly realized what had happened and hospital staff were able to save the prisoner from a critical overdose of methadone and morphine. We have learned through the years that there is nothing an inmate will not consume or try in order to achieve a release of his pain or to otherwise just enjoy the high he or she may be able to obtain by combining various substances.

chapter four

The worst living area in the prison is called segregation. This is where I found myself working from 2011 until 2014. Segregation is a unique area of the prison with small and very basic cells usually holding just one inmate, but occasionally two. Segregation is a prison within a prison for problematic inmates. Only high-risk inmates who have a discipline problem and pose a threat to themselves or other inmates are confined in segregation. Segregation inmates are allowed out of their cells for just one hour during each 24-hour period. The majority of inmates spend six months or less in these solitary confinement conditions before being returned to regular penitentiary status.

However, there is currently a young First Nations man on the east coast who has been kept in segregation for the last 52 months. His name is Aaron Carpenter. When he was 19 he was arrested on minor charges and sent to jail. It was there where he got into a fight with another man who died from his injuries. Carpenter has been waiting an incredible four years for his trial, a time frame we see way too often at the Pretrial Center as well.

While he has been waiting, he has been kept in solitary confinement, in a glass box, in an empty cellblock with no windows, and with the lights kept on for 24 hours. Carpenter has interacted with so few people over the last four years he is losing the ability to speak. I personally saw this identical situation day after day while I worked in segregation.

Counted in days, Carpenter has been in solitary confinement for 1560 days now. To put this in perspective, consider that the United Nations has declared this form of segregation should never surpass 15 days. They did this because it is considered one of the worst forms of psychological torture.

It is unknown exactly how many other cases there are like this right across Canada and the USA but in

Ontario, Canada's chief human rights commissioner identified 1,383 cases of prisoners being held in solitary confinement for more than 15 days and twelve of these people have been subjected to this for more than a year.

If this happened in a country that is notorious for violating human rights, like Saudi Arabia, we would be outraged. Discovering this is occurring in Canada and the USA is initially shocking and difficult to process.

If a prisoner with mental health issues is kept in segregation for more than 30 days, the provincial minister responsible for correctional services must be informed yet clearly this is not creating any results. When questioned about this specific case, the provincial minister stated, "That is a decision that is made by the individuals operating our jails. I will not take individual action on a specific circumstance."

In the case of Carpenter and many of the other mentally unwell individuals that have been stuck in segregation right across Canada and the United States, there are readily available solutions. St. Lawrence Valley Correctional and Treatment Centre back east and Colony Farms Forensic Hospital in the west are specifically designed to house and treat prisoners like Carpenter who suffer from mental illness and may pose a threat to themselves or others.

Colony Farms Forensic Psychiatric Hospital is a secure, 190 bed facility that treats and rehabilitates individuals who have come in conflict with the law and are deemed unfit to stand trial or not criminally responsible due to mental illness. The goal is to restore fitness to attend court proceedings and reintegrate patients gradually and safely into the community. It also serves individuals transferred temporarily from correctional facilities to be assessed or receive treatment for a mental illness under the Mental Health Act.

However, the problem with these facilities is that they are also overcrowded and underfunded just like the prisons themselves. So while Carpenter and the many others like him belong in a forensic hospital where they can get the treatment they so desperately need, overcrowding and bedload capacities force them to remain in the segregation cells in which their mental states worsen even further.

In segregation, I got to interact with a variety of these 'special' inmates on a daily basis. Perhaps the longest term of these inmates was that of a man who was later convicted of stabbing his wife and daughter before submerging them in a river inside a piece of black luggage. Serial killers became my personal favorite inmates because of their ability to converse. This inmate had explained to me, many years prior to his conviction, that he had not committed the crime. He spoke so smoothly and convincingly. Like a used car salesman. Or internet scam artist. At times, I felt like I was being sold an object, perhaps a piece of luggage and at other times, I caught myself actually believing him until I pulled myself back to reality. Psychopaths are able to speak and act in a way that continues to baffle and amaze me. They can talk their way out of any situation, so calmly able to manipulate anyone to see things their way. These are the ones that often choose to represent themselves in court, truly believing that they can talk their way out of anything. Often, it was these sociopathic and narcissistic traits that finalized their fates - keeping them in jail forever. I truly believe that they often believed their own lies, however, that could never overcome actual evidence when it came time for their day in court. Another serial killer I had spoken to almost daily for more than two years had convinced me that he was, indeed, innocent of his multiple homicides. On the final day I saw him, he gave me a wink enroute to court, where he told the crowd about the woman he had murdered. I suppose the wink was him giving me a heads up knowing that the truth was about to spill out. Or, perhaps it was his style of mockery, his way of saying "I had you" after having manipulated me for the last two years.

I rotated working throughout the prison, from one living unit to the next. Lock-up schedules never changed; just the individuals within the walls did. On average, a total of 30 to 35 inmates inhabited each living unit, and each of the individuals belonged to the same gang. Occasionally they found themselves in the wrong unit, then ran to me and frantically whispered that they needed off the range. This meant the inmate had worn out his welcome with his peers, was mixed onto the wrong gang living unit or had simply broken one of the rules of the inmate code. It was either he get off of the living unit immediately or otherwise be forced to fend off a gruesome attack. Inmates often made weapons by sharpening any items they could get their hands on, ideally metal but plastic if needed. They used creative techniques in their weapon creating endeavours as well.

Perhaps the most gruesome was 'hot buttering' as the inmates called it. They would boil as much butter as they could and then add sugar, this mixture would be thrown into the face of their victim. The hot butter scalded their face and eyes but it was the sugar that melted into the victim's skin, literally melting his face away. The injuries were often life threatening but for the survivors, the scars were lifetime reminders.

I would order the inmates asking to 'check off' the living unit to go to his cell at once and close the door behind him, basically locking himself away from any of his predators. In this way, jail was very similar to an open safari. Prison is a zoo. The strongest survive and the weakest run, hide, or go into protective custody. If this issue continues in protective custody, the final guarantee of safety resides in segregation – locked away for 23 out of 24 hours a day and having zero contact with other inmates.

One of the few things inmates eagerly look forward to each day is his one hour of yard time. Guaranteed by law, for one hour each day inmates are moved from their living units through a series of concrete halls into an open concrete courtyard. Here, inmates can walk the 90-foot-long courtyard or shoot a semi-inflated ball into a basketball hoop – no netting, of course. Another option was to get an hour of natural daylight against their skin. The one-hour time slot was changed daily and never given to the inmates in advance so as to avoid devious plans of escape or drug drops. Along with three meals a day, this was as good as it got. Yard time was a reason to live; the only moment in their day they could even imagine they were not within the prison walls, the one moment that broke apart the daily mundane life they were forced to become accustomed to.

In segregation, however, all these 'extras' are eliminated – taken away like a parent does from a misbehaving child. The inmate's television and social hour in yard are removed. They are no longer allowed to order items such as chocolate bars and other treats from the jail canteen. Magazines too are forbidden in most cases so the inmate is left with nothing but themselves and their minds.

Segregation cells are completely bare; a 9-by-11 foot cell with grey walls and a black plastic mattress as a bed. The cell lights never turnoff so that the correctional officers have full vision of the cameras in each cell. A stainless steel toilet and sink combination are all that exist inside the cell. For many prisoners, these conditions often create such a severe mental illness and fatigue and they began yelling and chanting to themselves throughout the day and night. Occasionally these inmates would try to find objects such as sharp pebbles to harm themselves in what could be considered a last attempt to regulate their minds. At first mention of self-harm, the inmate's clothing was taken away and replaced with a suicide smock – a simple, sturdily quilted, collarless, sleeveless gown with adjustable openings. Along with losing their clothing, they would also lose their 2 inch thick mattress as well. Nearly naked and cold, this is when so many inmates finally understood what rock bottom is. This is arguably the lowest one can descend to in society and in life. Nearly naked, completely alone and being video-taped in a bare prison cell. Rock. Bottom.

However, it is here in segregation where I learned the capabilities of the human mind when pushed to its lowest levels. When humans are

39

caged in these conditions, something internally kicks in. It is like the brain finally realizes there is no longer a reason to live or any farther to fall, so nothing is out of the question. I witnessed inmates carving Nazi symbols into their bare skin with nothing more than a pebble they found on the floor. Often, inmates would cover themselves in their own feces and even consume their own excrement. Inmates would attempt to attack us by spitting on us and throwing their saved urine on us as we walked by. To the average person witnessing this would be followed by an immediate call to 911 with most likely a prompt referral to victim services. To a correctional officer in segregation, however, these were events that we had seemingly become so desensitized to that they were more of an annoying reason to do more paper work than anything else. And just as the prisoner's mind started to deteriorate, so did mine.

The initial normal feelings of shock or concern caused by witnessing these kinds of acts soon were surpassed by my feelings of excitement and enjoyment. I started to feel unsatisfied by a 'non-eventful' shift, so thoughts of intentionally kicking items that could be used to self-harm under inmates' cell doors became a pastime of mine. Spitting in the inmates' food before handing it to them became normal. Offering advice to inmates who had repeatedly failed when cutting their own wrists on how to make their effort more effective became a lesson I wished I could offer these types of scum. And just like their lives had hit rock bottom, I came to realize that mine had as well. So I started to drink alcohol, and lots of it.

Alcohol, I quickly learned, was an incredibly effective way to numb the body and more importantly, the mind. After a stressful day in segregation, a few glasses of wine would make me loosen my shoulders and throw away the lingering thoughts of inmates taunting me and the ghastly things I had witnessed over the last 12 hours. Alcohol became so effective that soon I had intentionally become an alcoholic. Often, people think of an alcoholic as a person who wakes up with a glass of scotch and stumbles around at home throughout the day because they are unemployable, but that was not my situation. I didn't drink in the morning but more often than not I required a drink to fall asleep each night. I, admittedly, did cope with alcohol. By 2013, I had become so dependent on alcohol that not having it would make me shaky. I had lost my first fiancée and was well on my way to drinking away Valerie as well.

Valerie rarely, if ever, drank when I met her. She battled hard but in short order I had her drinking as well although not nearly to my level, she didn't have the daily horrors to drink away like I did. However, as she went back to removing alcohol back out of her life, alcohol became a constant battle between us as she tried to take it out of my life as well.

At this point in my life, without alcohol I was miserable. I still went to work each day but the sober minutes ticked by as I waited to return home to the bottle. The previously easygoing Jamie had grown a hard shell. Inmates and staff started to notice this. Coworkers told me that I reeked of booze in the mornings. I realized that the vast majority of my coworkers were also heavy drinkers, to say the least. Most of our conversations revolved around alcohol and how drunk we had gotten the night prior. Once a week after work, on the last day of our four-on/four-off pattern, our group would gather together to get drunk at the local pub. From there, we would say our goodbyes as we watched each other drive home, some drunker than others. Perhaps it was our personal group counselling session because who else would understand what our days looked like.

chapter five

In November 2013, construction was completed and the new segregation unit at the Pretrial Center became operational. The new segregation was greatly enlarged; what was once just one floor was enlarged to three floors and the inmate count tripled from approximately 20 inmates to an excess of 60 inmates. The new construction removed the secured staff station, including the glass barrier that was used for staff protection, and instead placed segregation officers in the middle of the entire segregation unit, unprotected. Furthermore, during the tripling of the inmate numbers, segregation officer numbers did not increase. Although it was an extremely dangerous workplace beforehand, this new larger and unprotected segregation became mentally and physically unsafe for both staff and inmates and it created an even more hazardous and dangerous workplace for all involved.

In the previous five years, a British Columbia government report had shown that assaults on prison staff had increased by 18 percent; inmate injuries had increased by 70 percent, and violence between inmates had increased by nearly 50 percent throughout the jail.

While working in segregation, I was verbally and physically assaulted on a daily basis. At first I figured it was just the physical assaults that were cause for concern, but soon I would find that the verbal outbursts and emotional assaults were equally damaging.

"Campbell, eventually I will get out of this cell and I'm going to cut off your dick and then fuck you with it until you bleed," they would scream.

"Hey Campbell, your parents live in Surrey still, don't they?" they would taunt.

On February 3, 2014, in between the inmates' regular 30-minute checks, an inmate on the second floor used a piece of pencil lead to cause a fire in his cell. This process, commonly known in jail as 'sparking,' was accomplished by pushing a piece of pencil lead into the cell power outlet. This in turn created a small electrical spark that, with enough time and luck, not to mention the touch of a piece of toilet paper, would create a fire. Often this prohibited tactic would be used by inmates to light contraband cigarettes or other drugs that had been smuggled into the jail. However, on this day the inmate had a much more sinister plan in mind. This inmate created the fire and intentionally broke off the cell fire sprinkler head in his cell. On our control board at the staff station, I was notified of the smoking sprinkler activation. My partner and I immediately responded to the cell. Upon our arrival, we could see the sprinkler water flooding out from the bottom of the cell door. In addition, the cell was engulfed in smoke, restricting our vision. My partner and I made the decision to open the cell door, but in the heat of the moment we made a crucial mistake. Where were the inmate's hands? Was he holding anything? Were they empty?

I made a mistake that day that I promised myself I would never make again. The inmate's hands came swinging out from behind him and his cup of urine flew towards us. Thanks to my mistake that day, he nearly pulled it off with perfection. However, with a quick reaction that I had learned to rely on so frequently in segregation, I was able to sidestep the cup of flying urine that was destined for my face; instead I got it on the side of my pants. These were the types of games they played with us and the games we became ready to expect.

That night before bed, instead of drinking half a bottle of wine, I finished a whole one.

By this point, I had begun to experience constant night terrors while sleeping. It was not the first time I had encountered them, but it was the first time I realized just how severe they were getting. I was really starting to worry. They were often very similar in nature – walking on my 30-minute rounds around the three-level segregation. The dreams were so realistic. I often later compared them to the Hollywood movie *A Nightmare on Elm Street*. The sounds and smells were so vivid and the thoughts and assaults were so realistic. One night Valerie woke me as I was screaming for backup.

"Jamie, you're safe! Jamie, you're safe!" She repeated this until she was able to get me conscious. She explained what happened. I quickly went downstairs for a shot of whiskey and then went back to bed because I had to be up for work in three hours. I needed to be numb.

A few days into February, I stopped into my assistant warden's office. She was a 20-year employee within Corrections, although the vast majority of these years were spent in administrative roles. She now found herself in the actual jail, dealing one on one with both inmates and staff. She would never say it, but her fear showed in her eyes. I had told her that I needed out of segregation, that I was 'burning out.' Burning out was a common term that I often heard staff in the old segregation using when they could no longer handle it physically or, more commonly, mentally. Being yelled at, threatened, and assaulted on a nearly daily basis was not easy on the mind, and quite often staff lasted just a year or so before requiring a new post in the jail to refresh the mind and body. I had been working in the old segregation for almost two years, but it was the layout of the new segregation that officially knocked me out and put me on the mat. She told me to give her a couple of days to see what she could do. I did give her a couple of days, but just barely. On February 4 at 6:58pm, I wrote her an email:

"Hello. Just seeing if you found a new unit for me to work in yet? I am very desperate to get out of here. Each day is getting worse. Every passing minute here is like an eternity. I am praying, for my mental health, you find me a new spot ASAP. Thanks again, Jamie."

If I had envisioned what this new segregation layout would bring over the next two months, I would have certainly put even more urgency into that email.

chapter six

I was made to work in segregation for an additional two months after submitting that email, each day growing more and more anguished from the environment that I was being held in. These months seemed to pass extremely slowly and each shift felt like an eternity. During this harrowing period, I started to realize that I was falling apart both mentally and emotionally. I became severely depressed, angry, irritable, and generally unwell. However, I did not have the mindfulness and ability to comprehend or deal with what was happening. I could no longer cope with life's basic stresses.

My mental attacks became more and more aggressive and much more disturbing for Valerie and my family to deal with. I am very lucky that the worst of them only happened a few times a year. One moment I was perfectly fine and the next I felt a wave of nausea followed by panic. During this commotion, I could not catch my breath and I knew I was about to lose control. All I wanted to do was escape. The only problem was that the one thing I could not escape from was the very thing I wanted to run away from . . . *myself!* And inevitably these attacks occurred at a crowded restaurant or during a dinner party or in another city, miles from the sanctuary of my home.

I felt the panic build up, like a lion caught in my chest, clawing its way out of my throat. I tried to hold it back but people around me could always sense that something had changed, and they would look at me furtively, worried. *I am obvious.* I wanted to crawl under the table to hide until it passed, but that was not something I could explain away in public. I felt dizzy and often suspected that I would faint or become hysterical. That was the worst part, because I did not even know what it would be like each time – each attack bringing its own subtleties. "I am sick," I muttered to myself out loud, always unable to say anything else without hyperventilating. I rushed away, smiling weakly at the people staring at me. They try to be understanding but they don't understand. I run outside to escape the worried eyes of people who love me, people who are afraid of me, strangers who wonder what is wrong with me. I vainly hope they will assume I am just drunk, but I know that they know. Every wild-eyed glance of mine screams, "MENTAL ILLNESS."

My mental health was about to grow even worse on what started as an otherwise uneventful April shift in segregation. I glanced over at a set of our cell monitors. Each monitor showed an inside view of each of the individual prisoner's cells, like those of an animal's enclosure at a zoo. From this 12-inch monitor, I could see an inmate appearing to pry at his arm as a tradesman would in an attempt to remove a stuck nail. As a segregation officer, I knew two types of behaviors – natural and absolutely bizarre. There is no middle ground in segregation and this next event was to show me just how far an inmate could be pushed. I immediately attended the inmate's cell to get a better view of what was going on through his glass cell door. I instantly noticed a large amount of blood pulsing out of the inmate's left inner forearm and forming a puddle around his white prison-issue Velcro shoes.

The inmate was grinning as I made initial contact with him. As he turned to face me directly, he had a look of pride on his face. It was like a child showing his parents a completed school project as they entered the front door. The prisoner rotated, showing me the large gash he had created in his forearm as he continually used his two-inch prison issued toothbrush to dig deeper and deeper into his arm.

"Code yellow, code yellow!" I panicked into my microphone calling for immediate backup as my voice cracked anxiously. "Code yellow segregation!" I blurted again as I took my first step into the cell. Immediately, with a flick of his wrist, the inmate gauged his toothbrush into his arm causing his artery to shoot a spray of bright red blood at me and my segregation partner, who was now beside me. With the extension of my big black boot, the toothbrush went flying out of the inmate's hand and to the far corner of the cell seconds before I tackled the inmate to the ground. The inmate was restrained and then he received the emergency first aid he desperately required. Although I can only imagine the enormous amount of pain this must have caused the inmate as he carved deeper and deeper inside his arm, he smiled and giggled through the entire ordeal. My only guess would be a mixture of medication and severe mental illness.

That night, I pulled into my driveway trying to determine the wording I would use when Valerie asked me how my shift had gone. "Non-eventful day dear, nothing really to mention," I would lie through my teeth. "I'm feeling real good today, looking forward to dinner." The gruesome details I would leave for my mind to sort through like I always did. However, this night I would most certainly require the assistance of a stronger sleeping pill - whiskey rather than my regular bottle of wine.

By this point, my coworkers were starting to notice a change in my coping abilities and my irritability as well. During inmate medication rounds one afternoon, a nurse understandably demanded that I come back to healthcare with her to get my blood pressure taken. "Campbell, what's wrong with you today? All week, actually, you have seemed off. But you seem super agitated today." She paused. "And your skin looks red and blotchy – you don't look well." Before I could give her a lousy excuse, she gave me a head shake and I knew I was busted. I headed back to healthcare with her. That was the first time I had confirmation that my physical health was, indeed, starting to fail as well. My blood pressure registered 142 over 98 and with a shake of her head she flatly directed "You need a break from segregation. You are not looking well, and I don't think you should be in there anymore." I told her I would keep asking management and that was the last we ever spoke of it. However, that was just the beginning of people voicing their concerns. My coworkers and even my supervisor began telling me how they were seriously worried about me. And, it was just two weeks later that everything finally came crashing down. My deteriorating mental health continued to intensify as incident after incident occurred. This time, it was a physical assault.

On April 26, 2014, I was sent to do a hospital escort shift. Although hospital escort shifts were generally unpopular amongst the other correctional staff because of the boring nature of the work, I was greatly appreciative of any of these shifts that I could get. For me, it meant getting a one-day escape from the chaos that was segregation. However, I was about to realize that my luck was no better in the 'safety' of the hospital than it was in the hell of segregation. At 8:05 p.m., my inmate woke up from a deep sleep. He had been arrested just a short time prior, but he was suffering from severe alcohol withdrawal symptoms. As a precaution, the prison doctor had ordered him to be evaluated more closely at the City Memorial Hospital, which was not far from the jail. Although it was uncommon for inmates to be transferred out of the prison and taken to city hospitals, it did occasionally happen. Correctional staff would either drive the inmate in a secure transport vehicle or they would be taken by ambulance escort.

"Who the fuck are you?" the inmate demanded upon waking. His voice was shaky and still sounded drunk. "Answer me now, you faggot,"

His hands clenched and his jaw gripped tight. It was obvious he was not impressed with his present situation. His legs were shackled to his stretcher, but his hands were not cuffed, a decision I suddenly regretted. He continued to yell and curse loudly. Soon he drew the attention of other patients in our area, from whom we had tried to hide him.

"I am Officer Campbell and I am here with you to get you checked out by . . ." My sentence was cut short as he moved to spit at me. I continued to try to deescalate the situation, first with a quiet, calm voice. "I understand this must be scary for you to wake up in a new location, but . . ." Again cut off as he attempted to spit at me and rip the IV out of his arm. I tried a much firmer approach this time. "Inmate, I am giving you a direct order to obey my orders. I need you to lie down immediately . . ." The IV went flying and, although shackled, he attempted to kick me. It was at this time that I attempted to handcuff his left arm to the stretcher, but in the moment I took my eye off his right hand, he came across and landed his fist into my jaw. The punch was solid. My neck snapped sideways and the right side of my face started stinging. I was not knocked unconscious but I was stumbled from the blow. After a quick grappling act, I was able to get a hold of his right wrist and handcuff it to the stretcher, all in one motion. I remember feeling both rage and embarrassment as a few nurses started peering into our curtained-off area after hearing the commotion. "How did I allow this goof to land his fist so solidly on me?" I asked myself.

After I had gained control of the situation, I immediately notified the management back at the prison about what had occurred. My feelings quickly turned from raging embarrassment to worry, as it was common for officers to get suspended after incidents such as this. Management at the Pretrial Center often tried to avoid any responsibility involving staff or inmate injuries and would often use staff against other staff during the reporting of incidents. When I returned to the jail, I was sat down in the manager's office and asked to fill out an incident report. I knew to choose my words carefully.

It was just five days later that I would witness my first suicide jumper. One trauma rolled into the next and my mind erupted.

chapter seven

It could have been worse. Perhaps the mental health gods were trying to do their best for me that day. Perhaps they had been watching me slowly 'de-evolutionizing.' The once strong-willed, happy and social Jamie Campbell was now simply Officer Campbell and resembled more of an ape than a human being. Regardless, I was temporarily out of segregation and in a meeting in administration when I first heard the commotion on the radio microphone I wore across my shoulder.

"Code yellow segregation!" came shouting out of the radio from a voice I immediately recognized: it was that of my segregation partner.

Seconds later my heavy-breathing partner came back on the radio with obvious despair in his cracking voice. "Code blue segregation, code blue segregation!"

'Code yellow' emergency calls had become a regular occurrence on our microphones as prison counts increased; one or two in a shift was not abnormal. A 'code yellow' was called for any emergency situation. This ranged from staff assaults to inmates attacking each other. The code yellow announcement would be repeated over the prison intercom system, which was echoed into each living unit, hallway and room of the prison. All correctional staff would immediately respond and all inmates would be locked into their cells until the problem had been resolved and the code had been 'stood down.'

In my meeting with the deputy warden, at the announcement of the code yellow, he began bringing up the cameras of the segregation area. Although he rarely, if ever, entered the secure area of the prison, he liked to keep an eye on the staff at all times. This was one of the many reasons for the extremely low morale among the jail staff. Management was cruel and completely separated in both presence and awareness from myself and my fellow officers.

I inched forward on my chair to get a better look at the cameras as my heart began pounding within my chest. I had just left segregation before the meeting with the deputy warden just minutes prior; what could have gone so wrong so fast? Was my partner okay? My mind began racing . . . Had I noticed anything out of place on my last rounds? What prisoners were unlocked when I left? My thoughts were quickly dashed as the monitor zoomed in on a nude man lying on the ground in the middle of the common segregation area, where our unprotected staff station sat. I instinctively jumped out of my chair and began running back to my post.

It took me less than a minute to run back to segregation; control unlocked each of the nine secure doors as I reached for them. Moving around a prison is a slow process because of the large number of secure doors and gates.

However, control can automatically unlock them for staff responding in these sorts of situations.

My first views of segregation were the exact colored versions of what I had just witnessed on the black-and-white camera monitor in the deputy warden's office. A nude male was lying face down on the dull grey cement floor directly in the middle of the new enormous segregation unit. I could see that a small puddle of blood was forming around his head and that his right arm was bent backwards – his palm was up, but his body and arms were prone to the ground. I was the fourth officer on the scene and the other three officers appeared to be trying to communicate with the nude body. I took a knee beside the body and immediately recognized him as the same prisoner who had ripped his arm open and flicked his artery at me just weeks prior. He was not yelling, not even speaking. Instead, he was muttering incoherently. As additional officers began to arrive in response to the code yellow, the in-house nurses arrived as well, pushing the medical cart they brought to all 'code blue.' A code blue was any medical emergency currently taking place in the prison. The prisoner continually tried to lift his head, but because of the certainty of neck injury, we advised him not to move it. Eventually, we restrained his head to prevent him from moving it.

The nurses quickly took charge of the situation and tried to provide pressure on what appeared to be multiple large facial lacerations across his cheekbone and forehead. His right wrist was clearly broken, most likely shattered. A large amount of blood was forming under his body and around his head. An ambulance was immediately dispatched by my supervisor over the radio. I was directed to fetch the inmate a pair of 'reds,' the slang term for the all-red outfit each prisoner was made to wear inside the jail. I was then instructed to dress the nude, bloody body so that he could be rushed by ambulance to hospital. I put my blue latex gloves on my shaking hands as my adrenalin started to pump. Dressing the prisoner was difficult, as his reds continually got stuck on his blood-wet body. It reminded me of times when I had personally tried to get dressed without completely drying off after a shower. The water, or in this case the blood, just stuck on to the fabric making it difficult to pull up each of his legs. A couple of minutes later, the ambulance and firefighting personnel arrived and just like that, the inmate's puddles of blood were all that remained of the scene. Many of the other segregation inmates began to chant and bang fiercely on their cell doors; to them it was just another show.

Within a few minutes, there was a small gathering of officers who had responded to the code. We huddled around the segregation staff station. "Let's see it, let's see it, let's see it," a number of officers repeated, referring to the recording that we could access from our video system. Several times we viewed the video recording of what had occurred from each of the four cameras that had caught the "show." Why I did this I will never know, but these images are still ingrained in my memory to this day.

"That is truly fucked up," an officer blurted as he rubbed his eyes like he was trying to get dirt out of them.

"Nasty," said the officer to my right.

"Brutal. Just brutal," another officer said as he took a seat behind me, his head shaking back and forth.

The video showed the prisoner being escorted by two officers from his cell on the first floor to the entrance door of segregation. The inmate was clothed in a blue suicide suit because he was still on suicide watch after the previous artery incident with which I had dealt weeks prior. The suicide suit was a single piece of strong and indestructible material that was velcro around the body to create a sort of dress. It was meant to provide warmth and dignity to prisoners who were at risk of committing suicide. At the same time, it could not be tied therefore preventing strangulation or hanging.

The video showed the inmate dropping out from under the suicide suit and running, fully naked, directly for the staircase that connected all three tiers of the segregation unit. Just behind him ran the two male officers who had been escorting him. The nude prisoner ran up the staircase with the two officers in close pursuit. Just as the lead officer appeared to grab the prisoner, without hesitation the nude inmate jumped head first off the staircase like a swimmer diving into a pool. The inmate barreled down from the third floor towards the dark grey concrete. Perhaps it was because the inmate was overly medicated, or possibly just his sheer desire to die, but the inmate did not put up his hands in a last-minute act of self-preservation. Instead, his face made first contact with the unforgiving concrete floor, causing even the most seasoned officers to cringe.

The camera angles all showed a different perspective of the jump and the landing. Our cameras had been upgraded to high definition upon our move to the new segregation, so the once-blurry picture was now crisp and extremely clear to view. Camera 13 was mounted on the ceiling above showed the inmate making the initial leap without a second of hesitation. The side cameras, cameras 18 and 19, showed the inmate free falling in what appeared to be a peaceful and controlled free dive. Camera 2, from behind the staff station, showed him land face first. Not aware of just how jaded my life had become, I laughed alongside my fellow officers as we freeze-framed the exact second when his face made contact with the floor – the split second of flesh and concrete making first touch. As my mind had become so good at doing, I hid my internal thoughts by simply laughing at the entire process as I replayed it over and over and over.

Although this suicide attempt would bring me many months of agonizing nightmares, it also brought me the reprieve and freedom from segregation that I had needed so badly.

"Hey Jamie, you still wanting out of segregation?" the deputy warden smilingly asked as I walked into the secure area of the jail. "We can get you on the escort for the jumper if you want." He said it in a way that was very belittling, but I jumped on the chance nonetheless. Over the following weeks I was assigned back to the hospital to guard the inmate for whom I had provided hands-on first aid just seconds after his attempt at taking his own life.

Hospital escort shifts are mundane at the best of times and now I found myself watching over a machine-driven, unconscious body. The prisoner did survive his suicide attempt, but had broken many bones. His face was swollen, battered and a deep shape of purple. Over the following weeks, the inmate began his road to recovery and was eventually walking on his own. He had suffered a brain injury, so his speech and thought process were definitely impaired, and this alone brought tears to his mom's face during our first scheduled supervised visit.

Supervised visits in the hospital are perhaps the most dangerous times for a correctional officer. The walls that hold prisoners in a prison are the same walls that keep outside individuals out. In a hospital we did not have those walls. With nothing more than a baton and pepper spray, we are tasked with preventing the escape of the prisoner from within the hospital. Add to that equation the fact that the location of the prisoner is provided to the scheduled visitor, and the situation can become very dangerous.

During my time at the Pretrial Centre, only two prisoners had attempted an escape from these hospital escorts, but nonetheless it was a worry all escort officers were extremely aware of.

In this case, however, it was not an escape we had to worry about but rather a very upset family wondering how "we had done this to him." Over the next couple of weeks, during these one-hour supervised visits, the family spoke to me just as much as they spoke to their incarcerated family member.

"Why was he in segregation? Why was he not allowed to wear his own clothes? How did we allow him to jump from such a high platform?" The family grilled us about what "we" had done to him! Eventually the prisoner himself had enough of this line of questioning and scolded his family: "Mom, it's not his fault. Stop talking to him and talk to me," he demanded.

Perhaps he was just tired of hearing his mom's constant bickering or perhaps he actually felt for my situation; regardless, it stopped the ongoing verbal assault from his mother. Inmates and visitors were never allowed to make physical contact, but that day I made an exception and allowed them a goodbye hug as I watched streams of tears fall down each of their faces.

chapter nine

That next block of shifts I was scheduled back in segregation. Immediately upon arriving at my desk on May 8, 2014, I wrote another email to management, begging for a break.

"Hello again everyone,
I have clearly asked to be NOT POSTED IN SEGREGATION multiple times now for my own personal mental health. At this time, I am completely ineffective in here and I am mentally burned out of working in this post for the last 2.5 years.

For the last 7+ years working here, I have been extremely flexible with where I was posted but I am now asking for some understanding. Please just post me on any of the living units and let me have some time to get my mind back into working order.

Thank you. I appreciate your help.
Jamie Campbell"

That email brought me some reprieve. The scheduler began placing me in different posts throughout the building, varying from working on different living units, prowling the building as extra staff or serving as an escorting officer on the occasional hospital shift, guarding inmates who had been admitted for one reason or another. However, it didn't last very long. By this point I was again working regularly in segregation. My situation had become a joke in the prison amongst my coworkers and supervisors alike. Everyone clearly knew about my worsening mental health situation. I no longer had to look at the staff roster each day to know that I had been posted to segregation because as I neared the staff room prior to the morning shift, I would hear people whispering and speaking my name under their breaths. My fellow officers would pre-warn me by saying things like "Sorry buddy, they have you in there again" or "You are going to lose it when you see the roster." I had become nothing more than a joke.

My peers noticed my gradual mental dilapidation. But nothing changed. It was then when my first horrible thoughts began. I fantasized about entering the morning staff meeting with a bomb attached to my chest. Or hanging myself in the middle of segregation with a note stapled to my bare, bloody chest, stating in big, bold, black letters "I need out of segregation!"

My nightmares were becoming more frequent and they began affecting Valerie more seriously as well. She would all too often wake me with a gentle nudge, stating "Jamie, you are okay. Jamie, you are okay. It's me, Valerie. Jamie, you are safe." Once I had fully awoken, she would tell me that I had been sobbing in my sleep. Screaming sometimes, at other times just crying ferociously. She was beginning to worry for her safety around me while I was sleeping.

I also started to feel unsafe while I was asleep, unsafe while I was at work and even unsafe during my personal time. I was scared, very scared. And for the first time, I had now become unable to hide it all, even in front of the prisoners, against whom showing confidence was our main line of defense.

Over a 10-week period in 2014, just as I was dealing with my first thoughts of suicide, 13 first responders in Canada alone committed suicide. The reason? Post Traumatic Stress Disorder. The disease was taking lives by the handfuls and no one was listening or even aware of what it was capable of.

chapter ten

Prisoners are not necessarily geniuses but they are very aware of subtle change. I suppose being stuck inside a 9-by-11-foot grey concrete box with nothing more than a block mattress for 23 hours a day will greatly increase a human's senses. The prisoners began to sense my weaknesses and they began to prey on me. I had become the injured zebra trying to make my way through a herd of hungry lionesses. I was weak and vulnerable, and they could sense it. During my 30-minute cell checks, many of them would jump in front of their cell doors' eight-inch windows to see me jump back. The pleasure they gained from this was evident in their devious grins and cackling laughter. They would chant my name, which echoed throughout the gigantic segregation unit, just to see me cringe and my shoulders bow. Each moment in segregation felt like an eternity and even my fake facade began to crumble. Staff began to openly tell me that I needed a break and my direct supervisor told my long-time segregation partner in front of me that "I was close to a meltdown." He had seen it before and "I was there."

On June 10, 2014, I submitted a third email after numerous talks with management, begging for help. I was beyond my breaking point and I knew it. I knew I had lost control.

"Hello again,
I am sorry to keep bothering you but I am in such desperate need to get out of segregation – at least for a temporary period while I get back to normal.

Today again my life was threatened by an inmate and now two of the inmates in segregation call me by my first name. I have been assaulted in here one too many times and the daily verbal assaults and threats on my life are too numerous. My supervisor is even seeing a change in me and everyone around me thinks I need a break. Staff all around me see how my work ethic is deteriorating and my spouse is becoming worried about me.

As I asked a couple months ago, I just need out of segregation to get back to normal after doing 3 years in here. If I need to switch groups so be it. I do not even care where in the building I work.

I am okay working a living unit, or even in programs. I am even okay with hand washing the government cars out back if needed!

Please, please, please help me. I am literally turning into a mess here.

Thank you, Jamie"

I was convinced this email would be the end of my miseries. I felt like I had pushed a big red emergency button and my figurative white knights would swoop in on horseback to take me far, far away from segregation. I imagined I would be sat down and spoken with. I pictured them saying, with looks of honest regret on their faces, "Jamie, how are you doing? How are you feeling? Thank you for reaching out for help. We are sorry we did not offer you more support earlier. We are sorry for failing you as a government organization."

However, I quickly realized this conversation was going to be nothing more than a fantasy in my mind. There would be no conversation, no apology, no help and definitely nothing even closely resembling regret or remorse.

On June 16, 2014, six days after I sent that email, I came to work a battered and emotionally decrepit man. I walked in and accessed the three secure doors heading towards the roster board that showed where all staff were posted on a day-to-day basis. There it was: JAMIE CAMPBELL – SEGREGATION. The scowl on my face turned to rage as I looked down at my hands, which were twisting together violently. In fact, I felt like a volcano, bubbling slowly underneath an unspoken fury. I was about to explode with the red-hot lava of anger and contempt. I walked meaningfully to segregation that morning as thousands of thoughts and images raced through my mind. I was no longer Jamie Campbell. I was no longer a correctional officer. I didn't even feel human. If I had had a firearm that day, I can say with certainty what would have happened next:

That morning I would have acted normal, nonchalant and perhaps even easygoing as I walked into work. I would have stridden briskly to my desk in segregation, taking a seat in my regular comfy black chair. I would have said hello and exchanged pleasantries with whomever had been posted with me for that shift. I would have done my regular 30-minute checks on the inmates that morning as they continued to tell me about how they looked forward to 'raping me with my own body parts', as they often liked to inform me. I would not have said anything back, perhaps just replied with a smile. At 9 a.m., as management gathered at our unprotected segregation station, it would be then and only then when everyone would realize that I was not okay anymore. It would be then when they realized that they should have taken me aside and spoken to me about those emails, or the many times I had pleaded to each of them   for   help.

If I had had a firearm that day, the seven members of the management team at the Pretrial Center would no longer exist on this planet. I wonder if any apologies would have been given during that process as they begged for their lives.

Then, one by one, the 72 cell doors in segregation would have been cracked ajar and the now-cowering inmates would have been extinguished. I imagine segregation that morning being very loud as I went so methodically cell to cell and the inmates quickly became aware of what was happening to them one by one. However, the silence when I was complete would have been so peaceful and rewarding.

Fortunately, or unfortunately, I did not have a firearm with 79 bullets that day. Instead, I lifted my computer monitor over my head and screamed from the top of my lungs, with tears running down my cheeks, "Help me!"

chapter eleven

That day, June 16, 2014, was my last day stepping into that concrete warehouse of horrors. I headed to a doctor directly from work that afternoon as my mind raced and my heart pounded. I was sweaty and anxious. I needed help.

In the waiting room, my mind continued to bounce around as I questioned myself about what it was I hoped to get from my visit. The one thing I did know is that I could not go back to work the following day, so I started with that. The doctor, a lady in her 40's with blonde hair and a white doctor's lab coat, entered the room.

"Jamie Campbell," she stated with a smile as she entered the room, looking at my folder. "How are you? What can I help you with today?"

Prior to this I did not have a family doctor, so she was unknown to me but very welcoming nonetheless. The doctor listened intently as I told her why I was there and a few of the things I was going through. At the end she faced me, looked me in the eyes and stated bluntly, "Jamie, you're going to need a lot more than a few days off work."

It was in this doctor's office that I first heard four letters that would forever change my life: Post Traumatic Stress Disorder. The doctor told me she was certain that I had "it" and she got me in contact with a psychologist specializing in Post Traumatic Stress Disorder: Dr. Gayle Goldstein.

Just four days later, I made my way to this appointment to meet with Dr. Goldstein. One of her two offices was just a 30-minute drive from my home in the pretty community of White Rock, British Columbia. I had never visited a psychologist before, but my doctor had made it very clear that I needed to do so. And to be honest, even I knew I needed help.

The lobby of the office was empty and there was a small, neat note atop the desk, written in minute cursive letters: "Please take a seat." I stepped into the waiting room and gently lowered myself onto one of the two black leather couches. I reached out and grabbed one of the few information guides that had been laid out across the table. I skimmed through it and came across a page with the letters P-T-S-D in big, black, bold letters written vertically down the page. The page had bullet points listing facts along with a write-up about a firefighter's personal struggle with post traumatic stress disorder.

At the top of the page it stated boldly,

"Post Traumatic Stress Disorder is the fourth most common psychiatric disorder in the USA and 8 percent (28 million) Americans will suffer from Post Traumatic Stress Disorder in their lifetimes."

In cursive along the bottom of the page, a quote from Rachel Yehuda, professor of psychiatry and neuroscience, said of post traumatic stress disorder, "Once it enters the body, it stays there forever."

"Forever is a long time," I thought to myself, my brain trying to wrap itself around those words. It was then that I heard the door next to the waiting room open and the steps of someone approaching. A thin lady, somewhere north of fifty with dark eyes that sat on a soft face welcomed me into her office. She was Doctor Gayle Goldstein.

"Please, Jamie, sit wherever you please," she stated with a gentle hand pointing to numerous chairs and couches she had set up in her small but cozy office. I chose a love chair in the back and she pulled up her armchair in front of me.

"Well, I am happy you were able to make it out here today, Jamie. Doctor Ozolins sent me your file and I am pleased that you chose to come see me today." She smiled. I was nervous and spent no further time with pleasantries before getting into the details of what had brought me to her couch; nearly eight years as a correctional officer summarized in a 30-minute rant. She nodded as I spoke and I instantly felt that she was hearing what I was saying. During some of the nastier incidents I relived, she never cut me off nor displayed a face showing her displeasure with the hard truth of it all. Instead, she just listened. She listened to my words and felt my feelings. She heard what I was saying and understood my pain. Over the next 16 weeks, Doctor Goldstein became my outlet. She also became my defender. She confirmed my Post Traumatic Stress Disorder diagnosis and explained to me what the disorder was. I learned that PTSD is a complex disease of the mind. It causes intrusive symptoms such as re-experiencing the traumatic event. She explained that many people have vivid nightmares, flashbacks or thoughts of the event that seem to come from nowhere. She noted that PTSD can make people feel on edge all the time. Doctor Goldstein went on to say that sufferers startle very easily, have a hard time concentrating, feel irritable or have problems sleeping. They also may feel something terrible is about to happen, even when they are safe. I had learned that post traumatic stress disorder was a cruel being and I recognized all of its symptoms. It had me tightly in its grip.

chapter twelve

It was a warm summer evening in June when my older brother, Shawn, invited me to see a football game with him. Our local Canadian Football League team, the BC Lions, was hosting the Toronto Argonauts that night at the football stadium downtown. Shawn, married with two children, was now a successful high school vice-principal and a person I had always looked up to. Unfortunately for me, it was this evening I would realize how brutal my mental illness had gotten.

He picked me up few minutes past 5 p.m. Traffic

heading into downtown Vancouver was never a quick affair, especially on game nights, hence we had to leave very early for the 7 p.m. match. Upon entering the stadium, I immediately felt a surge in my awareness. So many people with so much movement making so much noise. People shrieking. Kids running. "Popcorn, get your popcorn!" a vendor called out as he bumped past me wearing a large plastic orange hat. My muscles all tensed without my consent. My eyes scanned. Was I back in segregation? Where was I? Was I safe? I backed up against the concrete wall so that no one could get behind me. "Hey, just give me a second, feeling a little messed up," I said to my brother, shaking my head. "Ahhh, I'm fine. I'll just meet you at our seats," I lied through my teeth. I was anything but fine.

He looked back at me, perplexed. "Okay, you sure?"

I nodded as if to say yes and began heading in the opposite direction. I needed a beer. Fast.

I made my way down to our seats and saw my brother sitting with a bag of popcorn on his lap. The look on his face indicated that he needed an explanation for the earlier illogical behavior. I handed him a beer. "I just wanted to grab us a beer," I forced a smile and lied again. I kept the other one for myself, my brother none the wiser that I had already guzzled a beer prior to making my way down to our seats. Alcohol, I had found, was incredibly effective at abating my mental surges. When my mind played tricks on me I had learned that a quick fix was to get a quick alcoholic drink. For a minute it worked again as we watched the ball soar through the air and the game started.

The attendance of the game that night was 23,210. It was announced on the big screen to the cheering of the crowd. Valerie also knew this number because I had texted her this number with a vague comment about the danger I was feeling. I felt as if I had 23,210 possible attackers. My eyes spent as much time scanning the crowd around me as they did on the game. I had not been in any crowds for quite some time, especially not one of this size.

"What's up?" my brother asked as he looked over at me sitting on only half my seat. I needed to keep an eye over my shoulder and at the spectators behind me.

"Nothing, nothing," I responded. "I'll go get us another beer." I smiled awkwardly.

This was the night when I realized my life had become a sham. What people saw in my face, my responses to their conversations – it was all just an act. My thought process was so flawed and my internal reactions were on hyper-drive all the time. Acting 'normal' was impossible. That night, I could not decipher between the loser and the winning team. I didn't even know the final score. As I managed my way to the nearest exit, my brain was inundated with sounds, sights, smells, and fears. Hundreds of people bumped into me and my mind took them as attacks. I began shoving back, yelling and defending myself. Over the next 5 minutes my mind fought off one 'attacker' after another. It was as if all the cell doors in the prison had come unlocked at once. I did not stand a chance.

My brother spotted me as a circle of people started to gather around me. He grabbed me by the collar and rushed me out of the emergency exit behind us.

By the time I got home, I was extremely agitated, stressed, and fatigued. My brother was astonished by the way I acted up in the crowd. He became even more worried about my behavior on the ride home. He demanded that we stop at my parents' house to decide what to do next. He felt unsafe taking me directly to my house. Valerie was working a night shift hence I would be alone.

My memories of what occurred during the next hour or so are scrambled and unclear. I was highly agitated and demanding to be taken home. My heart pounded and the artery in my neck felt like it wanted to jump out of my body. My first-ever thought of harming myself raced into my mind as I paced back and forth in my parents' living room. My mom began to sob and my brother and dad stared at me in shock, like they were witnessing the most horrific car accident. "We should all die here together tonight!" I screamed with both tears and anger fighting their way through. "We are a family and we should die as a family, goddamit!"

My mind completely failed me as thoughts of suicide ravaged through it. My psychotic mind made the deaths of my family seem marvelous. Two loud knocks on the front door interrupted my crazy rants towards my traumatized family. Two stocky police officers stepped inside. They wore the very same black holster belts that I had always dreamt of wearing.

It turned out that during my yelling about death and being together forever, my dad had snuck away and called 9-1-1. Two police officers quickly responded along with a local program called Car 67. Car 67 provides on-site emotional and mental health assessments and crisis intervention. As the police rushed in to confirm the safety of both my family and myself I collapsed in the living room sobbing wondering how I had gotten here. There was no place to go.

A police constable calmly requested that I join him to have a talk in the formal sitting room of my parent's home, away from both my parents and brother who stayed to speak with the second constable in the living room. As I sat, I realized that my shirt was soaking wet from the extreme agitation and the release of adrenaline. The Car 67 nurse took a seat next to me on the couch as the police officer stood by. I could hear my brother and my mom both sobbing uncontrollably from the other room. Each time I heard my mom's fearful cry my heart broke just   a   little   more.

The nurse was a short lady in her mid-forties wearing

her civilian clothing – blue jeans and a white blouse with little flowers patterned on the collar. On top of this she wore a black vest with the word POLICE in large, bold, white letters. I soon realized she was not actually a police officer like the other two officers; I spotted a Mental Health name tag on her lapel identifying her as Kathy. Kathy spoke to me in a very comforting tone.

"What's going on here tonight, Jamie?" she gently asked. "As you can see, we have been called here tonight because your family is worried about you."

I gave her a quick summary of what had become my life. She then explained her concerns about my mental health, especially regarding my suicidal and homicidal thoughts. I was speaking again when I saw her make eye contact with the officer standing beside us. It was at this moment I was interrupted mid-sentence. The officer asked me to stand up. He explained that they were going to take me to the hospital to get me some help. His face became very gentle, like that of a mother about to tell her children that their summer vacation had been cancelled. "I'm going to have to handcuff you now, Jamie," the officer said gently as he raised his eyebrows in his defense. "I know you are a correctional officer and I really wish I didn't have to do it, but it is our policy, so I have no choice."

As a correctional officer, for me, slapping cuffs on an inmate was a daily process to which I had grown accustomed to. The shiny metal cuff pushing down on the wrist, ratcheting the lock mechanism on the bottom and then back around. Now I found myself being handcuffed, an extremely foreign feeling to me. I first felt the metal as it touched my skin and then heard the clicking as the cuff tightened. 'Click...click...click', the metal was just touching against my skin as the officer squeezed one last time and the cuff seized up against my wrist bone.

As the second cuff locked onto my wrists, the immediate feeling of helplessness was overwhelming. The constable had allowed me to be handcuffed at the front of my body rather than from behind as usual. At least that created a slight ability for movement. My parents and brother gathered and put their arms around me in a group hug. "We love you, son," sobbed my dad.

I was walked down the driveway and out to where the police cars were parked – the driveway where I had spent so many hours of my teenage years playing basketball. This day would be a lot different from those fun basketball days. There were no smiles. There was no laughing. I was loaded into the back of a police cruiser and driven away as my family looked on, waving to me from the doorway, my mother covering her mouth in an attempt to hide her intense sobbing. Correctional Officer Campbell was now closer to being an inmate than he was to any part of law enforcement.

The back of a police cruiser is cramped. The leg room is nearly nonexistent and my already heightened sense of anxiety, fear, and anger tripled. I could feel my heart pounding out of my chest and sweat trickled down my back. I imagined this was how inmates must feel as they were being taken to the police station for booking. I thought about the inmates who had been loaded into this car prior to me – perhaps killers and rapists with whom I now shared my seat. Was the dried blood from these murderers now on my clothes? My mind raced. My heart pounded.

It was a short ride in the cruiser and the nurse did her best, leaning back from the passenger seat to explain to me what was happening and what I could expect. "Jamie, I know this is not easy for you, but I just want you to know that you have been detained under the Mental Health Act. You are not being arrested," she emphasized. "You are being detained involuntarily, however, until you can be cleared by a psychiatrist. This is a good thing, Jamie, I can promise you that," she tried to assure me. "We will get you to the hospital and lead you in as inconspicuously as we can. After which, we will get everything sorted out for you. I will do my best to stay by your side, Jamie, as we work this out," she finished with a smile.

However, once we arrived at the hospital, my worst nightmare began and all the calming words the nurse had said were thrown by the wayside. I was confronted by hospital security personnel along with a few nurses who briskly walked over to me as I entered the hospital emergency back door. They talked amongst themselves and demanded that I be strapped down to a stretcher using a four-point restraint harness. "This is for your safety, Jamie." "This is for the safety of the hospital." "This is just the hospital policy, Jamie." One by one, each of my four limbs was forcibly attached to the stretcher. I resembled a man back in the Crusades, ready to be tortured. One final belt was tied around my waist and to the stretcher, making it impossible for me to move at all. I felt beyond helpless. I am not suggesting that the hospital personnel treated me incorrectly that night, because I'm sure my erratic behavior made them feel it was for the best. Nonetheless, it was utterly traumatic. I was then stuck with a needle in my pinned-down left arm. Before I received the second round of medications that I was given that night, I was both physically and consciously incapacitated.

The nightmare continued the next morning. I cleared my eyes and slowly began to glance around. The walls were ivory and green. To my left, I recognized the stainless steel toilet/sink combo. I lifted myself off the black mattress on the floor. Although my mind was extremely foggy, I instantly knew where I was. I had been placed in a suicide cell, no different from the ones where I had spent so many years doing 15-minute visual checks on prisoners. A large black camera stared down at me. I did my best to regain my balance and I stumbled over to the big steel cell door. I pounded on the cell window like I had witnessed the inmates do for so many years when they needed a toothbrush, book, or otherwise.

The nurse came over and was surprisingly warm and welcoming, especially considering the situation.

"Good morning, Jamie. I hope you slept okay." She went on to explain that they had changed me out of my clothes while I was 'sleeping' and had bagged them up with all my personals. I suppose this explained why I was now dressed in light green hospital scrubs. My shoes, too, had been removed, replaced with grey hospital socks with a happy face on them. I stared down at my socks for a minute and wondered how they could be so happy. Whatever medications they had given me were clearly doing something.

"We will be by shortly with your breakfast and your medication." She smiled at me through the small glass window – my port to the outside world.

It did not take a genius to realize I was in the psychology ward of one of our local hospitals, Surrey Memorial Hospital. The hospital was being renovated and the psychiatric ward appeared small and old. As the day moved on, I was given a very basic hospital breakfast and my medication. By this point, they had me on a mix of anti-depressant, anti-anxiety, anti-psychotic and sleeping medications. There were also a few others for good measure. I felt like a walking zombie – unable to walk a straight line or complete a full thought or sentence. My mind was a vast, foggy mess.

At 1:30 p.m., my cell door was suddenly unlatched, the steel bolts crashing down on each other. Two large hospital security officers dressed in white and black uniforms led me to an office down the hall, where two doctors were waiting for me. "Good afternoon, Jamie, I am Dr. Jones and this is Psychiatrist Dr. Clemons. Please have a seat." The doctor motioned towards the only seat left in the room. "And now, Jamie, I will ask you, do we need these two to watch over you or are you feeling better now?"

Confused, I looked over my shoulder and instantly noticed the two security officers standing behind me. I had not realized that they were there. "I am fine. Totally fine," I slurred.

This appointment took over an hour. I went through my story, my entire story with corrections, moving into what had occurred the previous night. The doctor and psychiatrist had a thousand questions for me. The questions became a little overwhelming because of my befuddled mind but I did try my best in passing on any information I could. The psychiatrist explained to me that they were thinking about releasing me into care of Valerie and my parents. "I will be honest with you, Jamie," the psychiatrist began. "I do not think this is the place for you. In fact, being here could worsen your symptoms. But at the same time, I want to do whatever will keep you safe and help you get better. What do you think would be the best thing for you?"

It was an odd question; very odd since I was not expecting to have a choice in the matter. Did I want to be kept in a cell, sleeping on the floor and drugged to the moon? Absolutely not! So I kept it short and simple. "I think going home to Valerie and my parents is a good idea," I replied.

They stated that I would be required to continue some new medication and regular visits with a psychologist. They stated that they believed keeping me further would not be beneficial for myself or the hospital, which was at overcapacity. Within the hour I was dressed in my own clothing and in the backseat of my parents' sedan, heading to their house. Sleep was all I could think about and I was sound asleep in their guest bedroom within minutes of arriving. I had survived my first incarceration.

Just two days later I was back in an appointment with Dr. Goldstein. These bi-weekly appointments quickly grew from something I feared to something I looked forward to. Dr. Goldstein became an amazing outlet for me during tough days and someone with whom I looked forward to sharing my small successes with. Most appointments were held at her office in White Rock, which was closer to me, but occasionally I made the hour-plus trek downtown to her North Vancouver office.   On one Monday afternoon, Dr. Goldstein met with my entire family and Valerie. The support was amazing.

My relationship between my parents and I became very strong. Some days, I would make the trip to their Surrey home for simple coffee visits. At other times, we sat together for hours upon hours and dove into the dark side of post traumatic stress disorder and how it was affecting me. On a day to day basis however, Valerie became my rock. Her never-ending support, day and night, allowed me to make it through each day. She would always wake me so gently during my constant night terrors or support me in public when my mind was out of control. My worst symptoms had become depression, anger and a growing inability to cope.   This was referred to as a feeling of "powerlessness" – a word I would soon become familiar with in a mental health group that I enrolled in. It was a 16-week program, but I ended up doing it for 24 weeks because of my "need for continued assistance" – in dealing with many of the issues I had been identified with. It was a voluntary program, but it had been highly suggested that I try it because of my growing inability to deal with life's most simple conflicts, such as traffic or customer service interactions. These sorts of things – a simple traffic issue or a barista's mistake at the local coffee shop – would evoke a reaction in me that one would expect from a person confronting the killer of their family. Instantaneous aggressive and dangerous reactions became part of my daily life – throwing an incorrect cup of coffee back at a barista or following a driver to his house after he cut me off in traffic for example. I was clearly out of control. My stress level was through the roof and I was completely unable to regulate myself.

Stress came in many different forms. The worst, perhaps, was from my employer. Right from the day I had sent in my first sick note, they had been uncooperative, to say the least. Their actions and inactions while I was working in the jail had battered me into the mental health collapse with which I was dealing.

chapter thirteen

My last day on the job was June 18, 2014. But as summer turned to fall, I was still battling with both my employer and WorkSafeBC, to get the benefits to which I was entitled. On a daily basis, my struggle to get accepted for these benefits drove me deeper into depression and greatly increased my homicidal and suicidal thoughts. Between June 24, 2014 and August 20, 2014 I sent the Correctional Service a total of seven sick notes from doctors and psychologists. In each instance, these were refused by the employer without even a simple letter saying they had been not accepted. Rather, each of these doctor's letters, certificates, and notes were completely ignored.

Months went by and my bank account ran empty. Things were not going any better with my claim with WorkSafeBC, either. Putting forward a workers' compensation claim is not a simple process, especially for a mental health injury claim. Through the summer months and now entering fall and eventually into winter, I submitted document after document providing details of my diagnosed post traumatic stress disorder and major depressive disorder.

"When it's a physical injury, it's often easy to adjudicate," said Jennifer Leyen, director of special care services at WorkSafeBC. "If you're at work and you fall off a roof and hurt your back, it's pretty clear what happened. But when you're dealing with psychological injuries, we have to determine if it's work-related, and that gets very complicated."

Eventually, WorkSafeBC had me seen by its doctors, mental health clinicians, occupational health doctors, psychologists, and psychiatrists. It was not abnormal for me to have three or four meetings each week. And although each of these specialists evaluated me in a slightly different way, every one of them came back agreeing that I was suffering from severe Post Traumatic Stress Disorder with a secondary diagnosis of Major Depressive Disorder because of the trauma I had suffered while working in segregation at the Pretrial Center. However, my claim still could not get fully approved – that would take longer.

Fortunately, my parents were able to step forward to help me with my financial hardships throughout these months. Otherwise, my home would have most certainly been foreclosed on and I would have been both homeless and hungry. At first they offered me small sums of cash, but as the months passed they ended up writing blank checks so that I could keep up with my bills. They had always been emotionally supportive of me through this process, but it was also their financial support that kept me alive.

The Correctional Service made life unbearable for me. It appeared they were doing anything in their power to drive me to suicide. Between June 18, 2014 and August 12, 2014, the Correctional Service refused to reply to a single one of the nine emails I sent to them requesting information about why I was not being paid. I had gone two months without a paycheck. I tried emailing my assistant deputy warden and my deputy warden, but received nothing in return. On August 10, 2014, I decided I had no other means than to get in contact with the warden of the prison. I sat down at my home computer and began typing.

"Hello Sir,
Sorry to have to email you directly but I am running out of my options so I thought I would make one final attempt to contact you. Over the last 8-plus weeks I have tried making 8 attempts to get in contact with either the assistant deputy warden or the deputy warden in regards to my current absence. Neither one of them has contacted me back with even an acknowledgment of receiving my emails. I have been extremely patient in regards to receiving my pay and although I'm luckily in a financial state that money is not an issue, it is truly becoming a matter of principle that it is coming up to 8 full weeks since I have received a paycheck. I have been working at the Pretrial Center for nearly eight years and like to think of myself as a great worker to both staff and management alike; I feel like the true disregard of professionalism in regards to my current absence is unconscionable. I appreciate your time and hope that you're able to resolve this matter.
Sincerely,

Jamie   *Campbell"*

This email must have gotten the warden's attention because just two days later the assistant deputy warden finally made contact with me. She left a message on my telephone and quickly followed it up with an email just two minutes later:

"Good morning Jamie, I have left a message on your answering machine. As mentioned in my previous voice messages as well as emails. We have work available at the Pretrial Center to meet the limitations indicated on your most recent doctor's letter.
Please contact me as soon as possible so we can discuss   further."

This email and telephone call absolutely set me off. I tossed the laptop off my lap like a child throwing a tantrum. Why were they doing this to me? Where was the professionalism I should expect from a government agency? I ached internally. My heart pounded and my breath struggled. I could not control myself; I needed to write back immediately. I picked up the laptop, which had survived the toss, and immediately pounded the keys, one stroke at a time:

"Hello, I received your phone call 12 minutes ago and your 9-second voicemail. However, I have been instructed to have all my correspondence with you through email. You mention previous messages, however, this is absolutely false.

I have a record of all voice messages and incoming calls and I have not received a phone call from you for more than 3 weeks nor any voice messages. This print-out was provided by my cell phone network. Furthermore, as my accepted doctor's letter stated I am unable to attend work for any purposes. It stated "inability to focus and concentrate on work-related matters. Lack of energy to perform physical tasks. Inability to interact with other people."

I do appreciate your "attempt" to finally contact me, however, I feel it was nothing more than just another time delay tactic that I am becoming used to from the management team at the Pretrial Center. I hope to get some further information that is actually beneficial to my situation. Jamie Campbell."

It was a matter of seconds after sending that email that I was dialing my work union, the British Columbia Government Employers Union. I needed help and I needed help fast. My homicidal and suicidal thoughts were pulsating and for the first time I was not interested in calming them down. It was quite the opposite, in fact – I wanted heads to roll. Literally. My mind raced with different options of murder and how I would carry that out. The Assistant Deputy Warden and the Deputy Warden had to go. Valerie begged me to be peaceful. "At least go see what your union will do for you, for god's sake, before you do anything stupid!"

On August 13, 2014 I met with my union shop steward, Monique Wellford, for the first time. She was petite in stature, but she carried a great deal of strength and confidence as she walked me to her office inside the new union headquarters in Surrey, British Columbia. "It's a real pleasure to meet you, brother," she opened, continually using the term 'brother' as a show of union solidarity. "I wish it were under better conditions, but I have done some pre-reading on your situation and we will hit back hard, brother." I liked her vigor. It was a gorgeous day outside, but we were all business inside the union headquarters – no sunshine and daisies for us.

I left the office three and a half hours later feeling confident that change was going to happen. We had filled out a grievance and response to our Master Agreement article 19.0. The article regarded my benefits and demanded to finally find out why I was not being paid. I was fighting a financial benefits fight as well as a mental health fight and I was losing both. I was not sleeping and not eating. I was angry and enraged.

Just two days later, the employer notified the union that they were refusing my grievance and that I would continue without pay and benefits. No reasons were provided in a typed, shortly worded response.

"Dear Ms. Wellford. I have reviewed the circumstances giving rise to this grievance and the applicable language in the 17th Master Agreement. There has been no new information brought forth to provide support for this grievance; as a result it is therefore denied."

I drank that night. Heavily. I wanted the thoughts to go away, for my mind to slow down. I was so deeply hurt and angered that my own employer was doing this to me. I was begging for help more now than ever, and instead of a gentle hand, they kicked me down yet again. It felt like as I tried to protect my injuries they would hit me where I was vulnerable. Were they going to stomp on my head as I held my broken ribs? My head throbbed, my chest pounded. I cried. I screamed. I raged. However, nothing changed.

This back-and-forth ridiculousness continued day after day. On August 19, 2014, the Assistant Deputy Warden sent yet another letter:

"Mr. Campbell, the employer is extremely concerned about your attendance. You are directed to report to the workplace for a meeting to discuss your current absence tomorrow August 20th 2014 at 0900hrs."

This letter intrigued me more than anything. I printed a copy and held it over my head as I skipped around my living room like a man gone crazy. Was that happiness? I had not seen or felt happiness for a long time. One thing I did realize was that I was clearly doing a better job of hiding my serious mental illness than I figured I was if the people I dreamed of murdering were demanding that I meet with them. I thought long and hard about attending that meeting that day. To be walked into a management boardroom and have all the managers laid out for me around a damn table – it just seemed too good to be true! Like an all-you-can-eat buffet full of the finest cooking for a man who had not seen food in months. Luckily for them, Dr. Goldstein and Valerie intervened to prevent them from dying that afternoon. Apparently, not everyone was so unconvinced of my mental health. The management team was a different story, however; either they were completely unaware of the mental devastation they were causing me or they were enjoying it. Either way, they were doing a great job of it and it almost cost them their lives.

On September 3, 2014, I opened up a large white envelope with a letter inside stating that the Correctional Service had finally approved my benefits and reinstated my full salary. It had taken nearly three months to accomplish and had almost cost me my life, but I had done it. Or at least I had done *some* of it. The letter stated that it was covering my wage and benefits moving *forward*, but that it was not going to cover the previous three months. No reason was provided. It was just another low blow to which I had become accustomed from this vicious, underhanded corporation that I was up against.

chapter fourteen

I was still asleep at 11 a.m. on September 4, 2014, when my union woke me from my drunken slumber; shaking off the previous night's self-medication was always my first challenge for the day.

"Hey brother, sorry, did I wake you?" Monique asked.

"No, was just having a mid-afternoon nap," I blatantly lied. I could not build up the courage to admit the truth.

"Oh sorry, but I have some more bad news for you unfortunately, Jamie. I've been on the phone all morning with the bigwigs in Victoria and then your management back at the jail. They are now saying that they are not willing to accept all of your sick leave. I really do not know what to say, Jamie. I am really sorry. In my decade plus here, I have never seen them take such a strong stand. And this case is so strong for you; I honestly don't know why they are doing this to you. It almost feels like some sort of personal grudge they have against you. I honestly feel for you, Jamie. This has been a crazy ordeal and I don't know what else I can do."

"I think I am going to finish my nap, Monique. I just can't deal with this right now. I'll come by your office later maybe…" I slurred out of dejection, anger, and my hangover.

It was one hour and 23 minutes later when I was woken again by the vibrating of my cell phone. The call display showed a 1-800 number from the government. "This should be good," I muttered to myself in contempt. It was Angie, my government occupational health officer, informing me about all the same things Monique had already done, albeit in a less soft tone, and that there was nothing they could do for me either. I did not even say goodbye before I hung up the phone. I felt beyond hopeless. Why could I not just die to end this misery? I needed a sledgehammer to deal with my rotting watermelon.

Just a few minutes later, as I was drifting back to sleep, my phone rang for a third time that morning. "Hey Jamie, did I wake you?" asked a voice I instantly recognized as Bryan, a close friend.

"No, just having a mid-afternoon nap," I lied. Again.

"Interested in going for some lunch?"

We met at a local pub at 3 p.m. and found ourselves a nice patio spot on what was a sunny, warm day. We exchanged pleasantries and handshakes. It started nice. It was like old times. Happy. Sunny. But it wasn't long into our visit that things began to go sideways – fast. I excused myself when the government called, reporting more of the same, and then again when the union followed up. I remember walking around the parking lot of the pub, screaming into my phone as passersby stared and whispered about me. I am sure I did not look well, to say the least. "Jamie, relax!" I heard my friend yell from the patio a good distance away. Clearly, my volume was amplified. I saw him running towards me. "Jamie, what is wrong with you?"

From there, things *appeared* to deteriorate to the point of my being asked to leave the pub. I say 'appeared' because my memories of the next 24 hours are cloudy at best. My father's email to my therapist Dr. Goldstein would shed some light on what had happened that day and evening when I woke up the next morning. On the hard ground, in a white cell. Again.

"Hi Dr. Goldstein, this is Jamie's father. Your call was cut short as Jamie's phone dropped and the battery fell out. I was already pulling the car over because Jamie was completely out of control screaming and trying to jump out of the moving car on the freeway to kill himself. Between myself, Shawn, Valerie and his mother we kept him in the car and put the child lock on so he could no longer open the door. We made it to the hospital and got him into the emergency room. However, at the triage emergency during sign-in, Jamie became aggressive again, screaming and knocking over the nurses' computer monitor. Although he initially agreed to come to the hospital, he was clearly having a change of mind. Hospital security personnel needed to be called to detain him because we were unable to talk him down. Once admitted to the hospital, they placed

Jamie into a small cell where we were still able to talk to him through the secure glass window and tell him how much we loved him.
We will keep you updated as the night progresses. Thank you again for your help.
Wayne Campbell"

As I read my father's email, the details of what had happened become clearer. I had clearly lost it.

chapter fifteen

The Chilliwack psychiatric hospital is exactly as portrayed in television and movies – white, pristine, and orderly. Even peaceful and quiet at times, except for the noise from the odd wailing patient being convinced to take his medications. There are many rooms with beds for everyone; some of us had our own rooms. I had my own room, so I felt special until another patient explained to me that this just meant I was being observed extra closely for suicide. I suppose this explains why they kept forgetting to give me cutlery too.

The main common area had the secure nurse's station, where we would line up three times daily to get our little paper cups of medication. After washing down the pills with a separate cup of water and doing the tongue check, we were able to leave the 'med zone'. I was a walking zombie the entire time I was there; no ups, no downs. Just an odd peacefulness. My physical movements were slowed and my thoughts were delayed.

Some of the other patients that I later saw, were clearly on too high of a dose because they would often just sit on one of the many sofas, staring off into the distance as drool ran down their chins; absolutely numb to the world. The rest of the common area had small round tables on which to eat, play cards, or drink an excessive amount of apple juice. There was one television, which we all shared. The common area also had a sliding door that most of us were allowed to go through although you had to be at level 1 to go outside. The doctors and psychiatrists could raise you from level to level depending on your behaviour and your risk assessment. I came in at Level 3 but moved to level 1 the following day so I got to escape the indoors and go out to a large grass area at the back of the hospital. For the first day on level 1, this was where I spent most of my time. Summer had just ended, but the weather was still warm and dry, and walking on the path was very peaceful. Plus, I wasn't quite ready to meet the other walking dead inside.

This attempted self-exclusion came to an end as my first lunch was served inside on one of the tables.

"You new here, I guess?" my table mate asked abruptly. He was my around my age, skinny as a board and had a brown mop of hair. I would later find out his name was Peter, or Petey as he liked to be called. "Well, I've been here, hmmm, I guess a few months now off and on," he began to ramble.

"It's a great place, actually. We have a basketball hoop out back, and on weekends they give us pancakes." He smiled brightly. His speech delivery was very fast and I quickly learned that Petey enjoyed his temporary home. The scars on his wrists told a story of his past.

As we finished our ham and cheese sandwiches, Petey nodded for me to follow him. I did. Within a few minutes I had met his "friends". Their names I forgot as quickly as they told me. I introduced myself and when they asked me what brought me to the psych ward, I replied, "Just needed a break, I guess." After all, that was the truth. I did need a break.

I was lying on my stretcher bed staring at the colored roof tiles when the nurse came in. "Jamie," she stated very happily in a singsong voice. "You have a visitor!" Her excitement about me having a visitor made me think that most patients weren't so lucky.

My medication made me quite dizzy. Hence I was cautious as I moved quickly behind her and out to the common area. Valerie was wearing all green, her favorite color, and looked right at me. The right side of her mouth broke into an awkward grin.

"Hi, babe," I said nervously as I waddled over like a baby penguin, pulling at my oversized hospital outfit and making sure everything was where it was supposed to be. Truth be told, I was embarrassed. I was ashamed. Humiliated and uncomfortable.

I understand that partners in life are supposed to be there for each other in the good and the bad, but this was beyond that. I had failed as a person. I had been admitted to a psychiatric ward. I had let my family down and I must have embarrassed her because she, most assuredly, had never experienced anything like this before. My mind tried helplessly to guess what she was thinking about me. What was she going to do with this mentally unstable maniac I had become?

Without delay, she raced towards me and threw her arms around my shoulders. We started to cry with our heads buried deep into each other. Her embrace felt so comforting, so wonderful. It reminded me of my childhood, when my mom would tuck me into bed with sheets straight out of the dryer. It was safe. It was protective. This hug Valerie gave me was one of love, yet it was also one of protection.

"I love you. I love you, I love you" I stuttered and repeated not knowing what else to say.

"I love you too, Jamie," she replied, using my name like she did only when I had done something wrong or when she really meant it. I suppose this time it was for both reasons.

I took her by the hand, walked through the common area, outside through the glass sliding doors. She had a million questions and repeatedly asked how I was doing. She cared. We walked to the far end of the enclosed grass area, sat on an old wooden picnic table, and talked. I knew my conversation was not the best because I was so sedated, but she never mentioned it. All she would tell me was how good I looked even though I knew inside she was probably wondering what the heck I was wearing. It was just like any other day. Well, any other day before my mind had abandoned us.

I was discharged within eight days. Two psychiatrists stated that I was no longer a risk to myself or anyone else, and the treatment that would do me the greatest good was out in the community with various mental health groups. They provided me with a number of new medications to take regularly and also a large increase in my current dosages. The nurses wished me well as they watched me walk away with my mom, my dad, and Valerie beside me. We had made it through another one.

I got an appointment to see Dr. Goldstein the very following day and I told her of my adventures. She secured me with her words and once again, I felt safe. She is truly a magnificent psychologist and an even better person - a savior, one might say.

Over the next three weeks, with the help of Dr. Goldstein, Valerie, and my union, I got down to business. I filed various grievances with my union to settle the outstanding amount that the employer was refusing to pay. More importantly, I filed both a workers' compensation claim with WorkSafeBC and a formal Human Rights claim with the provincial government of British Columbia. The workers' compensation claim required submitting a 23-page application package regarding my injury and the circumstances surrounding it. The Human Rights claim included submitting a 14-page application regarding how I felt the Correctional Service had violated my human rights by continuing to post me in segregation after I had made them aware of the harm it was doing to my mental health. Both were similar in content:

"I have been employed with the Correctional Service for nearly eight years starting in 2007. During the last three years I've been posted in the segregation unit in the Pretrial Center which houses only the worst offenders. Only high risk inmates who have a discipline problem or a threat to themselves or others are confined in segregation. Segregation inmates are allowed out of their cells for just 1 hour per 24 hour period.

"In December 2013, construction of the new segregation was completed. The new segregation was greatly enlarged; 1 floor was extended to 3 floors and inmate counts tripled from approximately 20 inmates to approximately 60 inmates. The new construction removed the secure staff station glass barrier that was used for staff protection and instead segregation officers now were showcased in the middle of the entire segregation unit, unprotected.

"Although it was a dangerous work place before, this much larger segregation became both mentally and physically unsafe for staff and inmate alike and created an even more hazardous and dangerous workplace. On a daily basis while working in segregation, I was continually sworn at, and verbally and physically assaulted (fists, urine, blood, and spit). I also dealt with inmates' suicide attempts and various forms of self-harm and cutting their bodies on a regular basis.

"The environment is extremely loud because the inmates constantly bang on their cell doors, yelling and taunting staff with threats. When this constant abuse became too much for me to cope with mentally, management was unwilling to assist or comply with my repeated requests, both verbally and in writing, for some time away from posts in segregation. My coworkers, supervisors, and family noticed the deterioration in my mental health. However, management still refused to address my concerns and simply told me that this is how it is and that I had to "suck it up".

"My Post Traumatic Stress Disorder was caused by these events and was exacerbated by the way that I have been abused and neglected by my employer. Through management refusing to acknowledge and/or having controls in place to educate or eliminate Post Traumatic Stress Disorder and other common correctional mental health issues, this has created and then aggravated my illnesses."

These were extremely tense and traumatic days, but as I leaned on all of my support networks, I submitted each of the large packages of documents to both of these agencies. There was no going back, I realized, but I also knew that there was no going forward unless I evoked change. My nights were traumatic for both myself and Valerie, as I often found myself patrolling the house with baton in hand. Triple checking window locks and confirming the doors were double locked. During the days I became a prisoner in my own home as I was unable to leave the house as I figured I would be attacked again. I would startle so abruptly at the slightest noise and I was angry. Very angry and very irritable.

chapter sixteen

Growing up, I had always been the class clown; I loved the attention it would garner and enjoyed sharing a great joke. I often hosted house gatherings and encouraged all to attend. I had a small but very close group of best friends and I was definitely an extrovert. At parties I was the one in the middle of it all, the team captain when playing sports, and the one standing up in front of the class to present for my group. I loved being around people, and people enjoyed my company as well.

However, things were different now. I had isolated myself from all of my friends, coworkers and even some family. Furthermore, I would often find myself fantasizing about hurting people, complete strangers, when I was in public. Day and night I began clenching my jaw and my fists, on the lookout for the next target. I was no longer anyone's idea of a fun time. People no longer wanted to be around me; I had an air of darkness clinging to me and everyone could sense it.

My life became divided into two distinct parts, each with its own difficulties. During the day, just getting out of bed was often too difficult of a task to overcome. I would spend some days unable to move, my body feeling like it was encased in cement. My mind too had given up and my depressed and angry feelings made my body feel heavy. Some days I would sleep 17 hours, yet I was still constantly tired. Trying to leave the house took great will and more times than not, I would simply give up and go back to the safety of my bed. When I did make it out of the house, I thought out my exact routes and strategy for leaving the safety of my home. Malls and stores created a huge amount of stress and anxiety and were avoided at all costs. One early winter afternoon, I was picking up groceries at a local supermarket when I got the feeling that I was being watched. This became a common feeling I experienced and I often recorded licence plate numbers and details of cars and people. Perhaps it was true that people were watching me because my body had become so jumpy and irregular. I probably did garner many looks from bystanders. This specific day, though, I was sure I had been spotted and followed by an inmate; I had noticed a white male with tattooed arms and neck follow me into my local grocery store. He then seemed to follow me from one aisle to the next and as my anxiety soared I was forced to desert my buggy and race back to the safety of our home. I would have to explain to Valerie when she got home from work why there was no dinner that night. I become a pretty difficult partner to live with, to love, but Valerie was always understanding. She would take time to explain to me how she understood. I was – I am – a very lucky man.

Nighttime was no better; some nights were bad and some were hell. Often I would awaken to Valerie gently stroking my shoulder and whispering, "You're safe, Jamie. You're safe. You're okay, Jamie." The next morning, she would explain how I had been thrashing and yelling in the bed. One night she watched in horror as I got on my knees while asleep and began viciously making a stabbing motion into our headboard with my fist. Looking back, the nights must have been absolutely terrifying for Valerie, but she never complained once. I suppose she was too busy reassuring me that I was safe and okay.

A major part of my Post Traumatic Stress Disorder was my extreme vigilance and a feeling that inmates or their associates could attack at any time. I had nightmares about this most nights, and leaving the safety of my home was tough. It was around this time that I had started growing out my hair and beard in an attempt to change my appearance. In all my years working at the prison I had been clean shaven with a buzz cut. This was the preferred hairstyle because it created a tighter fit for when we had to don our gas masks if we were forced to use a large amount of gas to clear an area. Another way of dealing with my overwhelming feelings of attack was going across the USA/Canada border. We lived only a few minutes away from the border so this was an easy trip that offered me great relief. I knew that inmates or individuals with criminal records could not possess passports, so once across the border, I was safe from them. Valerie would often join me for these frequent 'escapism' trips and mentioned how relaxed I became. "Your shoulders look so much more peaceful, Jamie. I can see your whole body is more relaxed. It must feel so much nicer not having your jaw clenched!"

Another thing I had begun doing frequently was yoga and meditation at a local studio by our home. At first I felt uncomfortable being in a group, but I soon found myself looking forward to my class and seeing the regulars. I knew I was 'safe' there even though it was in public; after all, it was yoga and meditation. I figured inmates and criminal associates most likely didn't frequent establishments such as this. The class often included soft music and candlelight, and it was often the most relaxing part of my day for the 90 minutes it lasted. The benefit that I was receiving from these classes was the reason that Valerie and I had booked a trip to India. However, management must have caught wind of this planned trip because on September 24, Patricia Affini and the management team at the Pretrial Center penned me another aggressive email:

"Mr. Campbell, you are expected to remain in the province where you have access to your physicians care. Failure to comply will be viewed as non-compliance on your part and will be considered accordingly..."

The letter had one purpose and one purpose only – to stop me from going on a trip to India that Valerie and I had booked. It was more of the same type of controlling behavior to which I had gotten accustomed to from the dictatorship of the management team at the Pretrial Center. Really, if they were going to be transparent, the letter would have read something more like:

"To our lowly peasant, Mr. Campbell,
We forbid that you go on your vacation. If you disobey us, we will crush you. We do not care about your mental health or your wellbeing in general. However, if you return to work, and get your ass back into segregation like the good dog you are, we will forget all of this and keep you on as one of our hundreds of lowly employees.
Fuck you, your management team."

Over the next two weeks, I made four medical appointments at four separate offices. My goal was to get opinions from these medical professionals as to whether or not they approved of my planned trip and any other feedback they offered. I saw my psychiatrist, my psychologist, my medical doctor, and my mental health manager. All four wrote strong letters stating that not only did they feel the trip would not harm my status, but that by not getting away on this trip, I would delay my recovery.

"Jamie's travel will not interfere with his treatment, and it is expected to aid in his recovery," wrote Dr. Ozolins, my medical doctor.

"I am writing this letter in support of Mr. Campbell's upcoming trip to India. As his case manager, I feel not going on this trip could undo the progress that Mr. Campbell has made. I am strongly encouraging Mr. Campbell to take advantage of the opportunities for relaxation and skills that will be made available to him," stated June Harmann, the registered psychiatric nurse at my mental health center.

"I believe that time away would be beneficial to his recovery," simply wrote my psychiatrist Dr. Babbage.

And my psychologist Dr. Goldstein wrote a long letter in which she stated, *"In order to give Mr. Campbell a much-needed break from the current psychosocial stressors that are aggravating his condition, it is highly recommended that he take his planned vacation to India."*

On October 6, 2014, I wrote back to the employer, attaching these letters of support from my medical team. My trip would go ahead as planned. Or so I thought. Yet again, it would not be that easy; my heart sank into my stomach as I began to read management's quick reply just a few days later:

"Dear Jamie, we received your email dated October 6th, 2014. This letter is to advise you that the Employer's position remains the same regarding your benefits. Benefits will cease to be paid should you leave on your planned vacation to India.
Yours truly, Patricia Affini"

I was crushed. The same individuals who had single-handedly shattered my mental well-being were now taking away my booked trip, which was meant solely to get me away from the disaster of a life I was living, to let me escape the constant letters and emails bombarding what remained of my spirit and soul.

How could they do this to me? Surely my four medical letters of support were enough. Surely my BCGEU union would take on this management gang in my support.

Unfortunately not. Multiple meetings with the union did very little. Grievances were filed and I was told it could be a year or more to see any advancement in my situation.

I began actively contemplating revenge. These were no longer just thoughts of general anger, or fantasies, as the professionals refer to them, but rather clear and precise plans of murder.

I was such a broken soul, and frequent psychologist appointments, medication, and family support were no longer strong enough to keep me on the right side of the track. I began drawing a layout of the prison. The front door shaded in red, doors drawn in orange, and everything else in black ink. I began driving by the prison to take notes of which managers cars were there in an effort to learn their schedules. This was not going to be a random attack. Secretaries and my fellow coworkers would not be harmed. It was a precise attack against those who had personally been assaulting me, the management team. I would be seeking apologies from a certain few. Apologies that were genuine were what I truly ached for. I feared receiving fearful pleas instead:

"I'm so sorry Jamie," they would sob.

"Please don't shoot me again, Jamie, I'll give you whatever you want," he would plead.

The tall, bald one would try to hand me his wallet as blood began to gurgle between his quivering white lips.

"Your wallet?" I would yell back at this offer. "Are you fucking joking me? Do you think I'm here to rob you? Are you a fucking lunatic?" I would scream as I shot him again.

This is not what I wanted; well, not exactly. I wanted their blood to spill, but I wanted much more than just that. I much preferred:

"We are sorry for ignoring you, Jamie. We are sorry for ruining your existence by what we personally did to you in this building, Jamie. We are sorry for not listening to your pleas of help. We are to be held responsible for the way we kicked you down repeatedly when you came to our doorstep like a stray dog looking for scraps. We are terribly embarrassed and appalled by the way we have battered you mentally and emotionally over these last 14 months."

Perhaps they would be on their knees in front of me. Single file. Each taking turns speaking. Words they truly meant. Words that came to them so easily because they were so genuine.

But then what? What is an appropriate punishment for each of their sins? Each had washed their souls clean and begged for forgiveness.

In prison, when an inmate breaks prison rules, he is charged with a prison violation and brought down to an internal court hearing. At this internal court hearing, the inmate is asked whether he pleads guilty or innocent and gets to see all the evidence against him. If he is convicted, a manager overseeing the internal court process chooses the punishment. Often this is a set number of days in segregation.

Perhaps this time I should be the judge in the court process. With the guilty managers kneeling in front of me, the evidence could be shown for all to see. All of the emails and doctor's notes. And then, I would choose their fates. One fat man, one petite lady, and one large bald man on the end. Each in turn.

Convicted. Convicted. Convicted.

Four bullets later we could all lie there together. Finally, we would be even. The wrongs they had done mixing together with my blood. We would all be even. As the last of the blood drained from our bodies, we could even whisper a final "fuck you" to each other through the bright blood draining out of our mouths.

Instead, I failed. Wimped out. Pussied out. Whatever you want to call it, I didn't pull the trigger. I didn't arrive at the Pretrial Center at that determined time or access the three doors to the management offices with a stolen swipe card as planned. Instead, I caught my flight to India on October 13. Beaches, yoga, and more than anything, just not here. It was the flight the management told me I wasn't allowed to take. The break from the madness they said I was not allowed to leave. It was not that I was afraid of doing their jury duty that day; it was that I was not ready to bleed alongside them on that cold concrete floor. They had been running my life for quite some time and I wasn't going to go out with them telling me when mine had to come to an end. I would choose the end to my story. Not them.

chapter seventeen

India is not just a country, it is an experience. You can go to Germany and just see Germany. You can go to South Africa and just see South Africa. But India is different. India is an experience. The colors, the people, the flavors, the culture and the history. They are all mixed together to create an experience - The India Experience. Valerie and I had traveled all over the world, but India was just what I needed. From the moment we stepped outside the Delhi airport, my mind was too overwhelmed to think about all the danger I had escaped back home. We did yoga and meditation daily and it soon became something we craved after our morning chai tea.

For years, travelers seeking serenity and spiritual renewal have made their way to India's ashrams and retreat centers to learn the wisdom of ancient practices like yoga and meditation. There are many ashrams that offer disciplined daily meditation routines that promise visitors stress reduction, self-discovery and an escape from a busy urban lifestyle. Our search began in Rishikesh.

Rishikesh is a city in India's northern state of Uttarakhand, in the Himalayan foothills beside the Ganges River. We stayed in a very basic red clay building that overlooked the Ganges River and meditated overlooking it each evening. The river is considered holy, and the city is renowned as a center for studying yoga and meditation. Temples and ashrams line the eastern bank, a traffic-free, alcohol-free and vegetarian enclave upstream from Rishikesh town. This is what I needed and this is what I had come for.

I returned on November 13, recharged and ready for battle. My employer, too, had made it clear that they had no intention of letting up. I returned to both aggressive emails and letters. It seemed that this would end in either homicide or suicide, most likely both.

One of the letters in my mailbox was from another member of the cruel management team, Chris Mayer. A former security guard at an arena, he had an approach to management that had not changed in design from his previous occupation: intimidate and destroy.

"Failure to comply with these requests will be viewed as non-compliance and your benefits will continue to be withheld. Yours truly, Chris Mayer," he penned.

Asshole, prick, bastard . . . my mind searched for the appropriate label. Nonetheless, I continued to play along like the puppy they demanded that I be. I submitted yet another doctor's submission as evidence for my illness.

To combat this latest email, I went back to my doctor again and got a 5th doctor's note.
"Jamie, you must be joking me," Dr.Ozolins said when she saw me waiting for her in the examination room. I shook my head. "I have never seen an employer like this, honestly," she laughed. "This should cover everything," she said as she handed me a boldly written sick note.

"No longer able to work." "Severe Insomnia." "Must not work in segregation." "Inability to focus and concentrate on any work related matters." "Lack of energy to perform physical tasks." "Inability to interact with other people."

All of the doctor's notes had been very clear yet the management team continued to refuse them.

chapter eighteen

On March 17, 2015, I received a letter in the mail. It had been 288 days since I had escaped from my post in segregation. I held the white envelope with a WorkSafeBC stamp in the top left corner; my name and address were written in blue ink. I took a deep breath and opened it.

"Dear Jamie Campbell," it read. "This letter outlines my decision . . ."

Would this be the last straw? Was this the end of Jamie Campbell? Would my management slaughter map be put to use? Not today it wouldn't.

My eyes scanned fast. Left to right. "About your application . . . considered the following incidents as part of my adjudication . . ." And then there it was, on page three of the decision letter. "Based on my review, I have concluded that you meet the requirements of Section 5.1 of the Act and that you are entitled to compensation for a mental disorder that resulted from your employment."

It wasn't that I ever doubted the result, rather, it was the overwhelming feeling of having finally received the validation of my disorder. I felt a sudden rush of adrenalin through my body and I fell to my knees. Vindication. Finality. Resolution. My face felt flushed and my hands trembled. I felt like a boxer that had been beaten all night but had refused to give up. I was bloody, bruised and nearly unconscious but instead of quitting I had pulled myself up off of the mat and knocked my opponent out cold. It felt good but I knew the fight was just beginning.

Just four business days later, WorkSafeBC had another letter in my hand and I quickly learned that, at its roots, WorkSafeBC is an insurance company. Quickly my claim had nothing to do with my safety or well-being. And most certainly it had nothing to do with the safety issues in segregation. This was now about money. My claim was about money. To them I was nothing more than a number and money. No one cared. Not my managers. Not WorkSafeBC. No one. I was a number. An insurance claim. And I was about to learn just how much I was worth.

On March 19, 2015, I received another letter from WorkSafeBC:

"Dear Jamie Campbell. WorkSafeBC is dedicated to providing quality assessment and rehabilitation for workers who have been injured. Arrangements have been made for you to attend the following Post Traumatic Stress Disorder-Pilot Program on April 07, 2015 at Oxford Health Services Ltd. . . ."

The 7th of April came and I felt nervous. I had done a drive-by the previous day to scope out the location. I did not like surprises and this time would be no different. The building was quiet. However, the attached recreation center was buzzing with activity. It was Easter holiday. Oxford Health itself was a common-looking business front, recognizable only by the big lettering across the door. The day before, as I drove out of the lot, I had decided where I would park when I returned.

Unexpectedly, there was a large gathering of people when I made my drive-by an hour before my appointment. The clientele waiting to enter was exactly what caused me the greatest anxiety. A large white kid with a grey hoodie stretched over his head waited in front, aggressively smoking his cigarette. Behind him lounged two or three similar-looking sorts, each nastier and scummier than the previous one.

Most certainly there was an inmate here, I figured. A parolee? Warrants? Someone I had tackled in segregation? Or worse? Would I be recognized? I had spent the last year changing my appearance – my buzzed haircut and shaved face had been altered, my hair now fully outgrown and drawn to the side, my beard covering the lower part of my face. I was in disguise like Batman covering for Bruce Wayne.

The front door was unlocked by staff and the herd of scum pushed its way inside. I watched from the safety of my car until the lobby had emptied a little. I cared less about being a little late – my safety was more important, I told myself. Eventually I parked and slowly made my way inside with nothing more than my extendable baton as protection hidden in my jacket.

I sat in a small room, a round wooden table in front of me. Over the next three hours I made my way through a heap of documents, from personality trait tests to consent forms. I had begun to really detest filling out the personality trait tests because of the suicide and homicide questions.

#112. Have you ever thought or tried to commit suicide?
#204. Do you often contemplate harming or causing serious bodily harm to others?

These questions always begged for a simple 'NO' tick off, but being part of a WorkSafeBC's claim, I now figured I would be more honest. Short and to the point. But honest. "Yes I have."

I was then introduced to the Oxford Health psychologist, who introduced herself as Dr. Alison Bird. The therapist was the most petite woman I have ever met, almost to the point of appearing fragile. No larger than a child, really. In her 50's and with pale skin and striking red hair, she reached out her hand to shake mine.

"Hello, Jamie." Her voice matched her physical stature – soft and delicate. "Thank you so kindly for making it out today. The ladies up front said you have already made your way through the introduction package. So I just wanted to take a moment to introduce myself."

The plan was that over the next 16 weeks, I would meet with her on a weekly basis to talk about my return-to-work planning. I would also see an occupational therapist once a week throughout the program. It was a pilot program that WorkSafeBC had created to handle a growing number of mental health claims with the clear intent of getting injured workers back to work as quickly as possible. It was becoming very clear where they were heading with me.

Dr. Bird, however, was anything but a heartless insurance agency – she was extremely nurturing and kind. She soon became a big part of my support group and someone I looked forward to seeing each week. She brought me a certain calmness, at the same time and she was a great listener.

With the addition of Oxford Health, my week became very full. I often joked to Valerie and my family that I was the busiest unemployed person ever. I had Dr. Bird on Mondays, my medical doctor on Tuesdays, my anger management group on Wednesdays, Dr. Goldstein on Thursdays, and Josh, my new occupational therapist on Fridays. After my psychologist appointments with Dr. Goldstein, I would take long walks along the beach or walk the local forest trails; with the help of my therapists, I had identified those as my two "safe areas." Safe areas were places that allowed my mind to shut off. Places where I felt no threats of harm. Places that allowed me to feel free. Hyper-vigilance is one of the cornerstones of post traumatic stress disorder and it affected me incredibly. Outside of my house, my mind was constantly racing and my body was on the brink of meltdown. So two hours of peace was incredible.

My 16-week Oxford program was extended to 20 weeks because of my "slow improvements", but the weekly visits with Dr. Bird were priceless. An even more caring and kind woman than I initially thought, she had a real motherly way about her.

"Oh hi there, Jamie," she would whisper when retrieving me from the lobby in a separate area we had arranged so that I could avoid sitting with the public. She also let me use the back fire exit so that I could avoid shuffling through the busy front lobby entrance when our appointments ended. Like I did weekly with Dr. Goldstein, we talked about my week, both the good and the bad. I had been diagnosed with major depressive disorder as well as the post traumatic stress disorder.

The hallmark of Major Depressive Disorder is the amount of daily dysfunction that it causes. A person with this disorder may be unable to work, go to school, or socialize. Sometimes they are unable to engage in basic self-care routines such as showering or taking their medicine. Most frequently, severe sleep disturbance is present along with eating disturbance particularly lack of desire to eat. Extreme fatigue and lack of interest in usual activities are common. The most serious symptom of Major Depressive Disorder that is frequently present is suicidal ideation (wishful thoughts of death) which is sometimes present with suicidal intention.

Dr. Bird and I often noticed patterns in my mood – upswings and then crashes "just like the ocean," Dr. Bird commented. Rock-bottom weeks were tough because, except for my constant suicidal thoughts, I had zero motivation. Getting out of bed was a mission and getting anything accomplished was nearly impossible. Laziness and depression of this magnitude are two completely different things. I was not sitting in bed thinking about how great this was and enjoying watching television. Rather, I was sitting in bed plotting different ways to get back at the management team and then on killing myself. I was numb to the world, and my soul was overwhelmed with darkness.

However, even in the worst of times, other than when I was hospitalized, I never missed a single therapist appointment. I promised Valerie and myself that I would do my best each and every day to get my life back. These appointments represented that effort and were very important to me and my psyche.

The weeks went by and on May 8, 2015, Dr. Bird submitted a progress report.

"Significant Post Traumatic Stress Disorder and depressive symptoms, high levels of suicidal tendencies and anger," she wrote. "Particularly difficult to address his anger due to his perception that this will allow his employer to 'get away with it.'"

Perception!? Just perception!?

How was this a perception rather than a fact? My employer assaulted me mentally and then tried to walk away from the issue. How was this perception? I had begged for such a basic request – a short time away from my post in segregation – and instead was refused. On top of that, I was assaulted by the language in their tribunal response and emails, including a late affidavit response that just happened to arrive on my birthday. And this was just perception?

chapter nineteen

Kurt Brunt is a mean, unhealthy individual. Standing just five feet seven inches tall, and with a beer gut protruding nearly as wide, he communicated with me in a way that was always underhanded and cruel. A radio call from him to attend his office always garnered a "Are you in trouble? Are you OK?" from the fellow line staff. Kurt, however, never stopped to say hi, nor ask how anyone was doing. Rather, he criticized. During my seven-plus years of employment at the Pretrial Center, I learned to avoid him at all costs. In my final days, as my mind turned towards the dark side, my only thought about Kurt was how I was going to move his large torso. He drove an uncommon blue sedan whose license plate number I jotted down just days prior to my last days working at the Pretrial Center.

I soon was aware of his home address and, during my darkest of nights, I would watch from the street and through his blinds as he sauntered around his living room.

Murder is a lot different than homicidal ideation. Homicidal ideation is a term all my therapists liked to throw around. "Mr. Campbell has a strong homicidal ideation," they would write. "Jamie can get agitated and fantasies of homicidal ideation are frequent in his conversation."

But murder is NOT homicidal ideation.

When inmates would slit their wrists left to right, that was ideation. Ideation is pretend and begging for help. If a person wants to die, they slit north to south along the vein. The leaking blood actually creates lubrication for the cutting. The same thinking applied to taking 20 pills versus the entire bottle. This I knew too well.

But murder. Murder was real. I didn't have homicidal ideation anymore. No. I was just too pussy to kill. Too scared to spend life in jail – in segregation as a former officer. Ideation, no. Afraid, yes.

I would watch Kurt every now and then. I even built up the courage to sneak around back once. Through the back gate. Trembling like a little schoolgirl. Pussy.

I am sure my inmates would have taught me how to be stronger. What window to break and how. Top or bottom? Slider or not? Better entrance spot? Wait inside for him to come home? So many options, they would tell me. Next would be how to get on with the procedure, but after all, they were in prison – probably not the best individuals from whom to garner information.

I digress. I continued to see my psychiatrist Dr. Babbage, and on May 26, 2015, his report was blunt:

"Jamie is quite activated from his post traumatic stress disorder. He has hyper-arousal. He has significant nightmares and is told by his fiancée that his nightmares continue to worsen despite being on a large number of medications now. His mood is variably angry and depressed despite his medication being increased to treat this as well. He does have fantasy thoughts of harming some of the managers of the prison as he thought they did not recognize his illness and could have gotten him help sooner. Future Post Traumatic Stress Disorder groups will have to be with very selective clients as his level of anger can be quite high."

My next appointment with Dr. Babbage was no better. In fact, things were deteriorating quickly. Within a few moments of my arrival at the appointment, Dr. Babbage was walking me down to the emergency room at the Royal Columbian Hospital in New Westminster, British Columbia. Clearly, he did not like what he was seeing or hearing from me; he felt emergency intervention and psychological treatment were required.

The rain had begun to sputter as I entered the emergency room. He told me to have a seat and not move. He went to the front desk and I could overhear him tell the others, who had begun to crowd around, who he was. He pointed at me and told a short but powerful summary of why we were there. I felt safe around Dr. Babbage. He was my doctor, but also had become sort of a second father figure to me. A man who, I honestly felt, cared about my well-being. I wasn't just another number to him. Not even just another patient to him. I was Jamie Campbell and I was suffering from severe Post Traumatic Stress Disorder and Major Depressive Disorder and he was going to help.

Within minutes, he came back and faced me. I lifted my head, which had been staring at the ground. My mind was racing and my blood boiling. As usual, I was nervous and angry. A mix that had become too familiar.

"Jamie, they are making a spot for you here," he gently explained. He sensed the worry in my eyes. "It's okay, Jamie. I work with these people. They are going to help us."

Us? I was finally part of an "us"? It felt good. I had not heard those words in a long time. I had felt so alone for so long – from day one of this madness. This sound of "us" felt so good. I was not alone.

"Alright," I said as I began to follow my leader through the secure hospital doors.

I was kept in the emergency room for a short period of time until a nurse came and walked me through the hospital and into the psych ward. My clothes and personals were taken from me yet again and were locked in a locker. In exchange, I received a set of scrubs, with which I had sadly become accustomed and familiar with. This time I was not given my own room, however. It was explained to me that overcrowding meant I would have to sleep on one of the stretchers around the outside walls of the ward. The only privacy was provided by a nearly translucent sheet separating each of the sleeping patients. However, none of this mattered, as they had me sedated just minutes after my arrival.

"Good morning, Jamie." I half-opened an eyelid and grunted back. My head pounded like I had been drinking tequila all night. Was it a hangover? What had they given me?

"I'm Dr. Prabash and I have been looking at your file this morning. To say the least, this has been a long and terrible run for you and I feel for you. I truly do. However, as you may guess, we are not a place that can help you all that well, I don't think, Jamie. We could continue to sedate you and keep you here, but what will that accomplish?" he explained.

I again grumbled in agreement.

I ended up being moved to the psych ward that evening and was kept for two further nights before once again being released back into Dr. Babbage and Dr. Goldstein's care. I was given two new prescriptions for irritability and they had notified my family, who were there to pick me up.

Another hospital, another overnight stay in a psychiatric ward. Yet no help or positive outcome. This was becoming scarily familiar and I was wondering if I was ever going to get better.

chapter twenty

I have learned that every person in the world is located somewhere in the spectrum of mental illness. Many people barely register on the scale, while others have far more than they could be expected to handle. Even specific disorders are incredibly individualized. For example, my depressive disorder comes and goes. When it's gone, I have a hard time remembering how I could have ever felt as lost or numb as I get during those times. My stress disorder, on the other hand, is always with me and comes with all sorts of "bonus" disorders and phobias, like some sort of terrible boxed set.

I began to spend a significant amount of time with my parents, like a scared puppy huddling around its mother. Valerie was working her four-on/four-off shift pattern, so that meant 50 percent of the time I was alone. Being alone caused me fear. There was strength in numbers and I needed numbers. I was broken, sad, and afraid. I needed a team.

My medications had been increased again so now the act of waking up occurred in the afternoon and not the morning. I would pull myself out of bed and go through my morning routine in the house. Twenty-five minutes later I would be knocking on my parents' large wooden front door.
"Well, there he is!" They would always welcome me in like they were expecting me. I guess they sort of were – this was becoming the norm.

"How are you feeling today, Hun?" my mom asked as she leaned in for our regular welcoming hug. She would always follow this up with her own answer. Each day she would state, "Looking good today, Jamie," or "You look off today, what's wrong, dear?"

I don't think my "look" ever changed, but somehow she nailed it every time. It's amazing, what a mom knows.

That day I was a little off, she told me. And she was right. Again. My nightmares were hitting me hard. Sleep deprivation was making my mind play games and suicide was creeping back into my mind as one of my options. Up to this point, two things had kept me from killing myself: family and fear. The two F's. I didn't want to let Valerie, Dr. Goldstein, Dr. Babbage, and my family down. Just the thought of seeing my mom cry as police notified her broke my heart. Not to mention the cost of burning a body these days – I am sure it is pricey.

Fear was also a strong deterrent. Killing myself is a tough thought to wrap my mind around. The human body is meant to strive, and at a basic level to at least survive; it has lot of automatic backups in place to make it live. Previously, I had gotten around these by getting shit faced. I had learned that fear and inhibition are erased, or at least humbled, by whiskey. But I had promised Dr. Babbage that my drinking days were over. And this time, I meant it.

I had been late to the party, figuratively and literally, when it came to drinking. It started as college fun, but instead of reducing with age, my consumption increased with each shift as a correctional officer. "If

I wasn't drinking, I wasn't having fun," I would tell Valerie proudly.

But as one doctor report after another came in saying that my liver was taking a beating and that my body could not keep up, I started to take notice. "But all my coworkers were doing it" was a line I had used for years like a child but had began sounding stupider and stupider, even to me. I started to realize why so many of my fellow coworkers were heavy drinkers and alcoholics – our job drove us to drink in order to cope.

I slowly built up the courage to start writing outside the safety of my home. It started with writing for hours during the summer months in my parent's loft. I moved from there to the isolation of nearby parks, then to open and quiet areas of sand along the local beaches. In fact, it got to the point that I brought my writing book and black-tipped pen everywhere I went. China, Honduras, India, El Salvador, Costa Rica, Panama and the list goes on. This book has been constructed internationally because, just like my Post Traumatic Stress Disorder, it does not shut off. It follows me on sunny days and rainy days alike. On vacations and at home. It is my shadow.

However, I found my most challenging writing spot was at Starbucks, regardless of the location. I saw many people writing and reading in each one I went to, but it just did not work for me. My Post Traumatic Stress Disorder makes crowds and busy places extremely difficult settings – my heart racing, eyes scanning, ears like those of a bat, unable to filter background noise.

My window seat allowed me a reflective view of what was walking towards me from the outside, while the mirror by the coffee cup display showed me what was behind me on the inside. There was only one public entrance and I faced it. On this day, on the opposite side of the coffee shop, sat a man whom I eyed the second I walked in and chose my corner seat. His red and black star tattoo that sat behind both of his ears immediately alerted me to his being an ex-con. He appeared to be waiting for someone and took off his black leather jacket, revealing two full sleeve arm tattoos. He appeared to be 27 or 28 years old. My mind raced, but I did not recognize him. Another man arrived and they shook hands. It appeared to be an interview or a formal meeting of some sort rather than just two friends getting together. My ears perked up like an owl's, and even though they were a distance from me, I could make out their conversation like I was part of it. "Construction job looking for hard worker . . ." They shook hands and exited together. I looked at my phone and realized that I had just lost another 38 minutes of my life in an interview of which I was not supposed to be a part of.

The weeks and months rolled by. I took on the "house husband" role and made sure the house was spotless and dinner was ready when Valerie got home each day. I couldn't work at a conventional job, but I refused to be useless. Getting groceries was difficult, but Dr. Babbage had raised my medications so that I could leave the house. I also had containers full of Ativan, both in my car and on me at all times just in case of an emergency situation. I continued to see Dr. Goldstein and Dr. Babbage weekly and on September, 10, 2015, Great West Life sent me a small pack of forms to fill out if I still wanted to be eligible for extended benefits:

"1. Please describe how you spend your time on an average weekday.
"Each day for me is very different. Some days my medications keep me from getting out of bed and/or require daily naps. Other days, I try to write in my book about my journey and how the Correctional

Service, namely the Pretrial management team, has turned my previously great life into this mess. Each day is hard for me, some harder than others, but with the support of my family and spouse I am somehow still here today. I try to keep an organized household, lots of rest, lots of medical appointments and walks in the forest or at the water's edge when I can. It is not a good life but it is my life, and I am doing the best I can each day."

7. Please provide any additional information or comments that you would care to make to help us better understand your condition and the effect on your employability.

"It is only because of the negligent actions and non-actions of the management team at the Pretrial Center as to why I am currently not still working as a correctional officer. Furthermore my ability to find and keep gainful employment for the foreseeable future has been compromised. Further information regarding this negligence will soon be available for all to see, including specific names, dates, and events as I complete my writings that got me to where I am today."

On September 29, WorkSafeBC sent me for a Permanent Functional Impairment (PFI) assessment. This assessment is performed on an injured worker to determine the degree of physical impairment incurred as a result of the worker's injury. This examination provides WorkSafeBC with a percentage of impairment, which is later used in calculations of injury settlements.

Dr. Neil Friegbie, a psychologist whom I had previously seen, was ordered to do the evaluation. He had been sent my extensive file beforehand. I entered his office at 12 noon on the dot. He was there to greet me in person.

"Hello, Mr. Campbell, I am Neil Friegbie." He introduced himself without a smile, very doctor-like. "I am not sure what you were told about our evaluation here today, but I am contracted out by WorkSafeBC to do your PFI assessment. We are going to start by doing a personality trait assessment, like you may have done in school over the years, and then we will finish up with an interview and getting your details." He made it sound quite easy.

My eyes began to wander over his shoulder and through the large double window behind him. It was a clear day and a number of crows perched on a power line just outside the office window, staring back at me. Mocking me, most likely: "Another PFI; it's his fifth this week."

The personality questionnaires were five pages long and each was practically identical to all the others I had been required to fill out throughout the last two years from one office to the next. I *sometimes* find it difficult to perform simple tasks around the home. I find going into crowds *difficult*. I *never* miss a meal. *Yes*. No. *Three times*. *No*. *Yes*. And on it went.

Upon completing the final page and signing and dating the bottom, I handed it back to the doctor sitting in front of me.

"That was quick, Jamie," he replied.

"I've had to do a few of those, it's starting to become second nature," I awkwardly joked back.

We then moved onto the one-on-one counseling part of the assessment. These also did not frighten me anymore. Telling the truth is a beautiful thing – it is only when you are lying that keeping a story straight becomes difficult. Honesty from day one was what I promised. Two hours later, the doctor thanked me for coming in and said that he would get working on his report immediately. He stated that I clearly had severe Post Traumatic Stress Disorder and that his report would indicate that. We shook hands and I was free.

On September 3, 2015, Dr. Friegbie's report came back. I downloaded and printed out a copy. He had been harsh with my prognosis.

"The worker is moderately to majorly limited with respect to productivity under pressure, decision making, multi-tasking, concentration and focus.

"Working with the public would cause a severe problem. He is prone to irritation and inappropriate expressions of anger. His suspicion of others sometime borders on paranoia. His hypervigilance, suspicion and feeling threatened would significantly interrupt the flow of work.

"Mr. Campbell should not be working in any setting associated with a corrections facility or inmate population. He should not be working in environments where he is exposed to members of the public. This restriction is permanent."

On November 18, 2015, WorkSafeBC issued its clinical opinion of the report. It clearly was no longer acting on my behalf. This had turned into a battle over money:

"I do not accept the following limitation noted during your PFI assessment: 'working with the public would cause a severe problem.' Although this limitation was mentioned in the PFI assessment you have positively demonstrated the ability to interact with the public in various situations over the past year such as the ability to travel to India in October 2014 and Belize in 2015. Given that you have successfully demonstrated the ability to take part in these activities the noted limitation is not accepted at this time."

So, in other words, WorkSafeBC was disagreeing with its own psychologist's report. It was explained to me that accepting this limitation would greatly reduce my chance of finding work. I explained that this was not my issue. I also explained that the reason I could travel, as they had mentioned, was because it had been outside the country. I was safe there. Inmates had criminal records, and with a criminal record a passport could not be issued. They knew this. I had explained this to them on numerous occasions.

WorkSafeBC had clearly put on its insurance firm hat. My health no longer mattered. It was all dollars and cents. Its goal was clear – get Jamie Campbell back to work as quickly as possible regardless of the implications because it would cost them less money. I was going to need help.

chapter twenty-one

On November 25, 2015 I met with a lawyer at Gopal and Company. Just a 25-minute jaunt from my home, the large grey stucco building was easy to find. I met Mr. Gopal in the main boardroom, waiting for me as a receptionist walked me in.

"Mr. Campbell, pleased to meet you," he announced and simultaneously offered his right hand. "Today, we are going to go over some of the basics of what we can offer you," he continued. "All we deal with here are WorkSafeBC appeals. I personally oversee each case and I have a number of lawyers who will work on your case on a day-to-day basis. In other words, you and your case will get the hard work and dedication you deserve. We cannot guarantee success, but I can guarantee you my personal best."

By the end I was sold. I had done hours of research, and meeting the lawyer in person cemented it for me. We shook hands one last time, filled out some paperwork, and transferred some funds. It was official; I now had representation against a cruel and desperate insurance agency.

On November 30, just five days later, with the help of Dr. Babbage, we submitted my Canada Disability Pension application to the Government of Canada. The Canadian Pension Plan provides disability benefits to Canadians who are disabled and who cannot work at any job on a regular basis. Mr. Gopal explained to me during our meeting the importance of starting this lengthy application process, and Dr. Babbage agreed. He did not sugar-coat his findings. He gave them to me just as matter-of-factly, for inclusion in my application.

I celebrated New Year's 2016 with Valerie, her best friend Katie, my old work mate Jason, and their partners at our home in what was more of a get-together than a party. Nonetheless, getting together with others was a great break from the life of isolation I had started to live. We, six of us, had a great evening. As the clock hit midnight, I decided to stand up and make an unplanned toast to the future:

"I would just like to thank you for coming tonight," I started. "It has been a tough year for me, but I have a feeling that 2016 is going to be a great one. I appreciate your friendships and wish you all a great 2016."

On the outside I must have appeared jovial, if not celebratory, but inside my feelings were much more confused. Would 2016 be my breakthrough year? Would I finally pull myself out of the darkness into which I had sunk so far over the last few years?

The very next day I began to pen a letter to Deputy Warden Kurt Brunt, the individual who had been culpable for my years of darkness. I did not know what I would write, nor did I know the tone it would take, but my therapists had taught me that writing was therapeutic, so I did know this letter was going to be for me:

"Dear Kurt,
    I am sorry for not getting back to you sooner. I have been most busy as you must imagine. We

never got a final farewell but as that saying goes, better late than never. However, please do not mistake my physical absence as one and the same as being mentally absent. As my spiritually enlightening trip to the north of India taught me, the two are completely distinct entities. And to think you told me not to go. Kurt, what a mistake that would've been.

You cross my mind regularly but rarely in person. In a weird way, you have somehow taken on the personification of the demon in me.

Do you think of me as well? I am sure my name must have come across your desk in the last 2 years. Jeez. Two years, unbelievable right. That is more than 700 alive days as they call them. I worked so hard for you guys – a good soldier I was. And to think all I had was the disease of time. Can you believe that? I'm sure you must regret not having the chance to thank me one last time. There was another time I remember. Do you? It seems like it has been so long since we actually spoke. I speak to you lots but that is just internally. Sometimes I whisper to you but other than an odd glance you pay no attention to me spiritually.

The Correctional Service has been very cruel to me, Kurt. However, babbling on about that would make me no different than an inmate I suppose. Right? Perhaps an internal court in segregation is what I truly need. Maybe Patricia could come down and hold court for us. She is so well-spoken. You could tell me how great you are, how many years' service you have and how many sick days you have taken. It would be impressive. I'm so pathetic compared to you. I tremble and shake now too. You never shake.

The storm's cyclone like destruction – verily its terror has filled me full.
Because of it affliction in my nightly sleeping place,
In my nightly sleeping place verily there is no peace for me.

I digress. It has been nice to finally be able to make contact with you, Kurt. Sometimes I feel you and the long-haired one just don't see me, or perhaps better worded is that you see right through me.

See you soon.

Jamie and Hailey. I got a dog, Kurt."

Writing the letter was very emotional for me. I felt like it was finally my chance to push back. I understood the letter might never make it to his desk, but it did not matter. The letter was for me. It felt good when I dropped it into the mailbox that next afternoon and with it fell a huge weight that I had been carrying around for too long.

The calendar page flipped over. February brought a sense of promise. I had retained a lawyer. I had applied for my Canadian Disability Pension benefits, and my woodworking hobby was going well. In an attempt to keep busy and stay positive, Dr. Goldstein had gotten me to begin building handmade signs made of stained pallet wood and spray-painted with stencil art. I had never done anything like this before, but the hours flew by as I worked in the peacefulness of my basement. I'll admit the first few were not pretty, but with each new one I completed, the finish got better and better. I soon found myself selling them on a local bidding site. Truth be told, the supplies often cost more than the final product, but that wasn't the point. I was capable and productive again. I was making things with my bare hands, things that strangers wanted. The process not only got me out of bed in the morning, it also made me feel useful. I was gaining back my confidence.

Just as quickly as I had found happiness, it was sucked right out of me yet again. On February 5, 2016, I opened a letter from WorkSafeBC. My eyes raced left to right through the seven-page decision letter:

"This evaluation was performed to determine if you have any permanent loss of function as a result of your injury accepted under this claim. Attached is a copy of a memo dated February 04, 2016. This memo summarizes my assessment and conclusions. The findings indicate you have a disability and are entitled to an award. Based on these findings and all other information on file, your award is equal to 30.00% of total disability."

I sat momentarily in shock. No feelings. No thoughts. Then my arms began to shake. Not just tremble, but actually shake. Like a volcano bubbling deep within me and slowly making its way to the surface. Then the eruption arrived.

The glass coffee table went flying from the pristine living room into the equally tidy kitchen. Glass shattered and was spit in all directions across the rooms. The glass vase holding hundreds of colorful beads that Valerie and I had loved so much flew across the living room and into the kitchen like a football being tossed. Devastation inside me and all around me. I was utterly emotionally ruined.

Thirty percent is what they felt was an appropriate number. This would boil down to just over a thousand dollars per month. How would I exist on this? What would Valerie think? Ideas, thoughts, and confusion played bumper cars inside my head. I dialed my lawyer, but hung up on the first ring. I needed to call WorkSafeBC first.

Unfortunately, or fortunately, there was no answer at WorkSafeBC, but at 4:37 p.m. I left a message that I am positive got across the gist of my feelings at that moment. I was a wee bit upset. I took a deep breath and then called the lawyer. Their words of condolence felt contrived, but perhaps it was because they had seen this play out so many times with so many clients over the years. "We will fight back, Jamie," she ended. I hoped it would be with a bazooka. Maybe an actual bazooka.

Over the next week I mentally deteriorated further and further. Nightmares tore me up at night, and during the day I was a danger to both myself and the public. My mind would 'flick' and the next thing I knew, I was driving 140km per hour down the wrong side of the road with Valerie screaming beside me. After the next 'flick' I would see myself yelling at my mom and dad after I had flipped their couch. I was dangerous. I was scared.

At my next appointment, on February 13, 2016, Dr. Babbage certified me under the mental health act and I was brought to the Peace Arch Hospital in Whiterock, British Columbia. Valerie was by my side, assuring me that everything would be alright. My first night, I was forced to sleep in a cell room identical to the cells I had guarded back in the prison. I was told this was due to their protocol until I could be cleared by a psychiatrist. My room was complete with a one-piece stainless steel toilet and sink combo – nothing else except for a mattress on the floor and the camera staring down at me.

I was informed by the nursing staff that the psychiatrist I would need to see was not in that night, but another doctor would come by and see me. It was just under 30 minutes later when a blonde doctor wearing glasses low on her face came in to see me. She spoke about Post Traumatic Stress Disorder and how I was not the first correctional officer who had come in. I had a mixed surge of feelings – one of not being alone and another of feeling sorry for the others who had been in this same fight at some point. As the conversation came to an end, she put her left hand on my shoulder and thanked me for my work as a correctional officer. I was taken aback. No one had ever done that before.

The next morning I woke up to a lady's smiling face standing over me. My eyes were very blurry, but even so I could tell it wasn't Valerie's face. If I had not been so completely out of it, my first thoughts would have been, 'Who the hell are you? Why are you so close to me?'

"It's me, Jamie. It's me, Jamie," she gently called. She saw I was struggling with her presence. She began to make a hole through the barrage of items I had set up prior to going to sleep as a sort of fortress. Two rolling desks and four chairs were all I could salvage from right outside of my cell. Nonetheless, it seemed to be working well, as it prevented her from getting over to me. I continued to try sitting up on the floor. By the time I was fully seated, she had reached me.

"How are you feeling this morning, Jamie?" she probed.

"Pretty groggy," I replied, stating the very obvious.

The doctor had prescribed a new medication to help me sleep, and clearly it had done the trick.

The nurse had come to explain that I was being moved upstairs to the fifth floor, the psychiatric ward. She also told me that she had read my file and we had something in common. We had both worked at the same Pretrial Center, she had been a nurse there nearly a decade prior. "I just couldn't handle it. I don't know how you guys do it" she stated bluntly.

Moving upstairs to the psychiatric ward was promising news, she explained to me, because I would no longer be sleeping on a floor. She tried to tell me some other pertinent details, but my mind was not speaking the same language. Her mouth was moving, but I didn't hear a thing.

At 2 p.m., two hospital security guards and a psychiatric nurse woke me up yet again and rolled my nearly unconscious body up to the psychiatric ward in a wheelchair. I wasn't asked if I would like to walk, but just like the security officers, I figured it was just more 'policy.' I didn't mind it anyhow; I played it off as a VIP hotel wake-up service.

Our elevator stopped on the third floor and a waiting elderly couple moved to step on, but the security officers motioned for the couple to stop. The nurse asked them politely to wait for the next elevator. I really was VIP – or crazy enough to be kept separate. The truth is probably somewhere in the middle.

The psychiatric ward was nice, as far as psychiatric wards go, I suppose. I was shown to my private room, the VIP experience still continues, room 518, which, as was promised, included a bed. And an ensuite...well, sort of. A toilet without a lid. Close enough. It was a private room, the only one of the 14-bed ward. I am not sure if I got this one out of sheer luck or because of my homicidal ideation, but I would guess the latter. Regardless, it was mine. All mine.

The rest of the psychiatric ward had various rooms, some for staff and others for patients. A TV room offered a large collection of VHS movies, which I didn't realize still existed. There was a Ping-Pong room that had everything but a net. The nurse explained that it had been removed for safety reasons. Hanging themselves by a Ping-Pong net? I guess anything was possible. My favorite room was the piano room, where a very old wooden piano sat. The keys were labeled but this did nothing to help me, seeing as I had never played before.

Some patients appeared to get along very well, while others were quite the opposite. As my first-night dinner of what was called "sirloin steak" was being handed out, two female patients in their mid-60s began arguing. "So you decided not to bring me a French vanilla coffee, you bitch," a lady with curly white hair accused.

"I fucking forgot, I told you that. And if you weren't so damn old, I would pick you apart for talking to me like that, bitch. You are so lucky, bitch, just so lucky. I have a rule about hitting anyone your age," her aggressor fired back as she gritted her teeth and shook her head.

Without missing a beat, the other, older patient, a petite lady in her 70s sitting all on her own at the far side of the table, piped up, "I don't have that rule. Shut up, bitch."

Oh boy, it was official. I was at the funny farm.

Overhearing conversations around a psychiatric ward is an amazing and eye opening experience. Listening to people talk sounds like a psychiatrist talking with their patient. They understand the diseases. They know their language. It is almost a game, especially to the younger ones.

"Do you freak out often?" asked a young curly-haired teen trying to strike up a conversation with a girl his age at the communal table.

"Only when I need to," responded the girl amidst giggles.

They have bi-polar. They have a mix of depression and schizophrenia. According to them, they have it all. Including Post Traumatic Stress Disorder. Maybe they do, but I have my doubts as the boy whispers to the girl, "It's the best damn doctor's note in the world," and the two begin laughing.

They talk about the newest medications and lowered side effects like an average teenager chats about video games or the newest school gossip. And they do it all with a smile. To them it is all a game and they laugh loudly and openly. The psychiatric ward is their local hangout while for me, it is my last resort. My heart aches and I know that Valerie sobs for me at home in our empty bed.

Killing hours and days in the psychiatric ward is not hard. In fact, for me it's ideal. It was there where I wrote page after page of this book. It was quiet and calm at times and there were lots of places for me to sneak off to - little nooks in empty storage rooms or out behind the big oak trees in our outdoor space. They all offered me the much needed quiet space in which to do deep internal reflection and transform my dark mind to light. Many psychologists purport the benefits of solitude for healthy adults. This includes allowing your brain to "turn off" and unwind. It improves concentration, and makes room for self-discovery. Lastly, and perhaps most importantly for me, it allowed for deep thought and self-care.

My favourite 'writing spot' was in a dusty old storage room down one of the far halls that I often found unlocked. Inside it was filled with old bins and patient gowns, books and boxes. It was perfect. No disruptions and lots of privacy to find my own little piece of solitude. I grabbed a wooden chair and found a small little desk and took a seat. My eye immediately caught sight of an old wooden sign leaning up against the far wall with a ridiculous amount of lemons pictured on it. The lemons were still yellowish but the big white lettering had begun to fade away. "If the world gives you lemons, try to make lemonade."

And that is what I did. I decided to make lemonade. A lot of it.

Perhaps the teens feel the same pain I do, but don't have a book like this in which to release their pain. Laughter to hide their cries and hurt? Very possible. I guess, in the end, we all have our own methods to make it through the traumas we face. For the longest time I did it with laughter and a bottle of whiskey.

On February 16, 2016, I was granted my first temporary absence. It was for a maximum of one hour, but it was a marvelous feeling to be "free." We drove to the coastline of the Pacific Ocean. Valerie entwined her hand into mine, while my left hand held onto Hailey's braided black leash. The hospital was just a 90-second car ride from the sandy shores of White Rock Beach; from the common room in the psychiatric ward I could see the ocean. It was idyllic. Other than it still being a psychiatric ward.

But the moments of freedom skidded to a halt as I walked through the secure psychiatric ward doors and was motioned over to the open area of the glass office that the staff called home. "Hi, Jamie, welcome back," smiled an unnamed nurse whose gentle Asian features made her perfect for the position. "I am not sure if you were advised, but we did some room moves today. We had to move you over to 502," she said, gesturing to the other side of the ward. "Also, we packed up and moved your personal things you had in your room." Without missing a beat, she innocently dropped in a 'little tidbit' that would change my stay at Peace Arch Hospital for the worse. "And we packed up and secured your cellphone for you in our personal lockers."

What she was saying ever-so-softly was that I had been busted. It was a well-known rule that cellphones were banned in the psychiatric ward. Signs at the entrance to the psychiatric ward not only pictured this but also boldly stated it as well. NO

CELLPHONES. CELLPHONES MUST BE HANDED IN TO STAFF.

It was clear. Clear as crystal. I admit it. I had even lied upon my admission. "And Jamie, do you have a cellphone of any kind with you?"

"Nope," I lied through my teeth, knowing full well that the pinching in my groin was from the cellphone and charger squishing together in my underpants. Jail does not teach a person many skills, but how to smuggle a cell phone through security was one of them. Although in jail it was often even further 'concealed.'

So here I was, without a private room and without my phone. No goodnight words from Valerie or soothing words from parents reminding me that I was okay. My safety blanket was gone.

On February 18, 2016, my regular rescue squad came and retrieved me. My father, my mother, and Valerie were standing in the lobby as I was released from the psychiatric ward yet again. It was deemed by the psychiatrists that support in the community was better for me than being stuck in a psych ward. I could not have agreed more. The four of us walked away from the hospital that day, arm in arm. Tears of joy trickled down my face – I was a very lucky man.

chapter twenty-two

I continued to see Dr. Goldstein and Dr. Babbage on a weekly basis. Each week brought new ups and new downs. On March 18, 2016, Dr. Babbage submitted my progress to WorkSafeBC:

"I have not seen Jamie for two weeks as I have been on holiday. Jamie has not seen his psychologist Dr. Goldstein either. He describes having more anxiety since not being able to speak to anyone. He says his family cannot tolerate some of his extreme levels of emotionality and reactivity. He is extremely interpersonally sensitive. He's had more nightmares

recently. He says because of these two factors he has started drinking alcohol to self-medicate. He does take medication at night for nightmares which has been partially effective but he also had to increase the dose. He takes 8 milligrams nightly. He also takes medication for depression and anxiety daily. He takes Ativan 1 milligram once or twice a day as well. He says the alcohol consumption has made him more angry and labile and he is motivated to stop drinking. He appreciates that it will make all of his anxiety and interpersonal problems worse. He does have passive suicidal thoughts but no imminent intent to self-harm. He still has fantasies of revenge regarding his old employers and prison managers but he says these are fantasies only and he does not plan to act on them. He is still working on writing a book. He's worried about his relationship with Valerie, his fiancée. He has become quite reactive and labile and angry towards her. He feels she is going to burn out and leave him. He has major depression which is partially treated with the above medications. He understands he must not misuse alcohol and his abstinence is the best approach. He agrees to this. He needs to be regularly monitored and receive ongoing psychotherapy and pain medication management."

And that is my story – to the current day. I will let you in on a very private secret of mine now, one that would have changed the ending entirely. My plan was that the day I finished writing this book, I was going to hang myself with a copy of this book hanging around my neck. It was going to be my final farewell – my last statement. But in the last three months, I have reconsidered. I originally decided on this suicide idea in the summer of 2015; at that time, I felt it would be my only way of showing my management team at the Pretrial Center what they had done to me. However, over the last number of years I have realized that this would not show them anything. They would continue to move forward like I had never existed. So instead I will continue to live and tell my story loud and clear. I will try to help others who have Post Traumatic Stress Disorder and who are in the midst of their battle. I will join Post Traumatic Stress Disorder conferences and support runs all over the nation, starting with the Pacific Region Walk and Run next week to promote awareness of this extremely dangerous disease of the mind. I have joined a crisis line to help others in their times of crisis. And I am just getting started.

Instead of dying, I will live. I will not just exist; I will grow and become a positive force. I pray that my story will create change in not just my correctional facility and my management team, but in management teams and facilities all over the world. There are currently thousands of first responders – police, paramedics, correctional officers, and firefighters – all over the world who are secretly battling their demons. Overdosing on pills, planning on where they will hang themselves, swallowing bullets. If you find yourself in this dark place, I want you to know that there is support and that I personally stand beside you as your comrade. You are not alone. Post Traumatic Stress Disorder is real and Post Traumatic Stress Disorder is scary, but together we can help each other through our struggles.

I am not cured. Nor is my life marvelous. But I am alive and each day I work very hard and try to become the best person I can become. I work on putting my puzzle back together, one piece at a time. Maybe one day I will not have daily psychotherapy appointments or be on eight different types of medication, but that is for the future to tell. All I can do now is take one day at a time. I will never again work in corrections or get back to where I was before all of this happened, but I will do the best I can each and every day. Maybe one day I will be able to relax and enjoy life without letting the fear and anxieties keep me from living the life I want to live. I am not there yet, but each day is a new day and each day I grow stronger. I continue to do what I do because that is life and because one day I may get used to all of this change.

Maybe one day I will have the same reaction to life that I have when I am walking along the beach – peace and relaxation without the debilitating feeling of fear and anger. Maybe one day I will acknowledge the frank truth . . . that I have no other choice but to breathe and move forward.

I have spent the last three years attending various mental health programing and extensive counseling in my attempt to get stronger each day. I have seen huge gains in my ability to cope with this world that we live in as I try to coexist beside Post Traumatic Stress Disorder and no longer run from it. I am closer to my family now than ever before and the writing of my daily thoughts has been the most therapeutic experience of my life.

I recently was finally notified by my lawyers that I had been victorious with my case with WorkSafeBC and I am excited to put that stage of my story behind me. My lifetime financial award will not solve everything but it does greatly validate the battle I have fought over the last three years. The award has removed any financial stresses I will ever face and it will greatly improve my quality of life. Most importantly however, it has put an enormous amount of pressure on the management team at the Pretrial Center and the Correctional Service in general. Hopefully no other Correctional Officer will be treated in the way I was or have to deal with the constant abuse that I had to endure from management for all those years in segregation and continuing while on I was off on my injury leave.

As for my future, that story is yet to be told. I am working closely with WorkSafeBC in furthering my education so that I can pursue a new career when the time is right. Helping others is something that I am certain I will do for the rest of my professional life. As I write this, I am working on my application with a local university in order to get my social work degree. I look forward to helping others through their battles one day through this work especially in regards to their mental health and the traumas that they are going through.

I am currently enrolled in yet another mental health program, this one is an eight week long Stress Management group program. It is held on the other side of the long glass hallway that I could see from when I was held in the psychiatric ward at the Langley Hospital less than a year ago. I suppose I have made it to the other side literally. In the program, we work on dealing with our daily stresses and on understanding themes such as the ability to identify the difference between stresses and stressors. It is nice being able to talk with others battling with similar issues and Valerie says she is already seeing a difference in my coping abilities.

After I complete this program, I will be immediately enrolled into a much more advanced 10 month long program called Dialectical Behavior Therapy. Dialectical Behavior Therapy is a much longer and more in-depth therapy designed to help sufferers change patterns of behavior that are not helpful, such as self-harm, suicidal ideation, and substance abuse. This approach works towards helping people increase their emotional and cognitive regulation by learning about the triggers that lead to reactive states and helping to assess which coping skills to apply in the sequence of events, thoughts, feelings, and behaviors to help avoid undesired reactions. Dialectical Behavior Therapy assumes that people are doing the best they can but are either lacking the skills or influenced by positive or negative reinforcement that interfere with their ability to function appropriately.

Dialectical Behavior Therapy is a modified form of Cognitive Behavioral Therapy, the type of therapy that I have been doing with both Dr. Goldstein and Dr. Babbage for the last few years. Cognitive Behavioral Therapy was developed in late 1970s by Marsha M. Linehan. This Cognitive Behavioral Therapy over the last few years has truly helped me in beginning my recovery but it is our hope that Dialectical Behavior Therapy will keep moving me forward as my treatment seems to be slowing. Dialectical Behavior Therapy is used in a variety of psychological treatments including Post Traumatic Stress Disorder and combines standard cognitive behavioral techniques for emotion regulation and reality-testing with the addition of concepts of distress tolerance, acceptance, and mindful awareness largely derived from Buddhist meditative practice.

My written story here now ends but my real story is just beginning. My name is Jamie Campbell, and I am a survivor.

Epilogue

In June 2013, a compelling report conducted by the Desert Waters Correctional Outreach Foundation was released. This extensive report overseen by Professors Michael D. Denhof and Caterina G. Spinaris found that more than twice the number of Correctional Officers suffer from Post Traumatic Stress Disorder than even battled hardened military veterans.

The report found that 34 percent of Correctional Officers reported suffering from symptoms of Post

Traumatic Stress Disorder, such as repeated flashbacks of traumatic incidents, hypervigilance, insomnia, suicidal thoughts and alienation. This was compared to just 14 percent of military veterans suffering from the same symptoms.

The estimated lifetime prevalence of Post Traumatic Stress Disorder among the general population is 7.8 percent.

Correctional Officer suicide rates are 39 percent higher than all other professions combined, according to a national study by professors Steven Stack and Olga Tsoudis of Wayne State University. A 2009 study by the New Jersey Police Suicide Task Force found that Correctional Officers had double the suicide rate of police officers.

And lastly, multiple national studies have shown that the average Correctional Officer will not live to see their 59th birthday. During my seven plus years at the Pretrial Center I went to three co-worker's funerals. One of these co-workers retired on a Friday and was dead by Monday. Correctional Officers are living mandatory death sentences, we just don't know it.

Acknowledgements

If it were not for a small handful of individuals, I would not have been alive in order to write this memoir to share with the world.

Firstly, and foremost, I would like to thank my beautiful and strong wife Valerie for her never-ending support of me. She hugged me when I needed a hug and supported me when I was at my weakest. The terror that I have put her through over these past 3 years I will never be able to forget but I look forward to the many positive years that lie ahead for us.

I would like to thank my family for their daily counseling sessions and for their unconditional love. Their support throughout this ordeal was so greatly appreciated and helped me move forward through my trauma.

And lastly, I would like to thank my medical team. It was only through the amazing work of the mental health professionals in the community that I was able to identify my disorder and then start the lengthy process of fighting back against it. I literally owe my life to you. Specifically, Dr. Laura Ozolins for originally identifying the severe Post Traumatic Stress Disorder that laid within me, Dr. Gayle Goldstein for her endless hours of therapy and unweathering kindness and to Dr. Christopher Babbage for his bold and honest appraisal and therapeutic support of me.

For more information about Post Traumatic Stress Disorder, please visit www.ptsdassociation.com or www.ptsdusa.org

Made in the USA
Charleston, SC
06 February 2017